FORGIVING OURSELVES

FORGIVING OURSELVES

Getting Back Up When
We Let Ourselves Down

WENDY ULRICH

DESERET
BOOK

SALT LAKE CITY, UTAH

Library of Congress Cataloging-in-Publication Data

Ulrich, Wendy.
  Forgiving ourselves : getting back up when we let ourselves down / Wendy Ulrich.
       p. cm.
  Includes bibliographical references and index.
  ISBN-13: 978-1-59038-857-0 (pbk.)
    1. Self-acceptance—Religious aspects—Christianity. 2. Forgiveness— Religious aspects—Christianity. 3. Church of Jesus Christ of Latter-day Saints—Doctrines. 4. Mormon Church—Doctrines. I. Title.
  BV4647.S43U47 2008
  234'.5—dc22   2007048475

Printed in the United States of America
R. R. Donnelley and Sons, Crawfordsville, IN

10   9   8   7   6   5   4   3   2   1

For Dave
Plus qu'hier, moins que demain

CONTENTS

INTRODUCTION

THE CHALLENGE

*There is a mighty power of healing in Christ, and . . . if
we are to be his true servants, we must not only exercise
that healing power in behalf of others, but, perhaps
more important, inwardly.*

—President Gordon B. Hinckley[1]

You might remember the story: During a famine, God sends
Elijah to a widow for sustenance. The widow ruefully tells the
prophet that she is preparing to cook the last of her food for herself and her son before they die. Elijah asks her to share with him,
promising that if she does she will never lack for oil or grain. As
pledged, she has enough to last through all the years of famine.

But the story takes a bitter turn. Despite the miracle of the
bottomless barrel and cruse, the widow's son becomes ill and dies.
Grappling with this wrenching loss she says to Elijah, "What have I
to do with thee, O thou man of God? art thou come unto me to call
my sin to remembrance, and to slay my son?" (1 Kings 17:18).

That's how it often works, isn't it? We get by, try to do what's

1

right, cope with life's challenges. But should something happen to someone we love, should our good fortune turn sour, suddenly it gets personal: "So this is about my sin, isn't it? Here is my failure coming back to haunt me. This is my punishment at last." We don't know what sin vexed the widow in the story (whose son Elijah soon restored to life), but we know intimately the sins, failures, mistakes, and frailties that vex us, challenging our claim to peace.

Although Latter-day Saints are among the best people I know, they are also among the most self-critical. Too often we work hard to improve and repent and then fail to fully claim the "amazing grace" of Jesus Christ. As one individual noted about a good Latter-day Saint friend, "She would take responsibility for war in the Middle East if she could figure out how."

As a psychologist and as a Church member, I've struggled to help clients, missionaries, friends, and colleagues let go of excessive self-blame and like themselves again. I too have spent many hours in that "dark night of the soul" that is haunted by the ghosts of my lesser self. This book attempts to map the journey from self-blame to self-forgiveness for fellow travelers, as well as for the bishops, therapists, family members, and friends who support us.

AN OVERVIEW

While our repentance ensures God's forgiveness, we need more than repentance to forgive ourselves. We also need accurate assumptions about the purpose of life and the place of sin and failure. We need to make sense of our past, fix our relationships with other people, and understand how self-forgiveness feels. We may need to update our beliefs about how to stay safe, change our expectations of ourselves, or get off the teeter-totter of shame and pride. We might need spiritual and psychological healing, not just behavior modification, before we can fully receive all that the Savior offers. This process of claiming God's and our own forgiveness can be summarized in four concepts that loosely organize this book: (1) clarifying our beliefs, (2) qualifying for forgiveness and grace, (3) overcoming internal obstacles to peace, and (4) trusting God.

Part 1 of this book, "Clarifying Our Beliefs," will review key elements of the plan of salvation (chapter 1), define self-forgiveness (chapter 2), and explore ways self-forgiveness can be an act of righteous living that benefits others as well as ourselves (chapter 3).

Part 2, "Qualifying for Forgiveness," helps us understand when repentance is called for (chapter 4) and reviews the steps of repentance (chapter 5), including changing behavior, making restitution, apologizing effectively, rebuilding trust, and forgiving others.

Having repented, we may still bog down in excessive self-recrimination because of unhealthy personality styles or difficult experiences from our past. Part 3, "Overcoming Internal Obstacles to Peace," looks at excessive shame or pride (chapter 6), depression (chapter 7), obsessive-compulsive, or perfectionist, tendencies (chapter 8), resentment and self-destructive unselfishness (chapter 9), and the effects of abuse or trauma (chapter 10). This section will help us see how self-blame gives the illusion of working for us while it hurts us in the long run.

Part 4, "Trusting God," reminds us that even when our sins are serious (chapter 11) or hurt those we love the very most, such as our children (chapter 12), the Atonement can bring us peace. Chapter 13 concludes with suggestions for exercising agency to truly choose God as our God by deciding to trust His capacity to love and forgive us.

WHAT TO EXPECT

So is there really light at the end of the dark tunnel of regret? I believe that no matter who we are or what we've done, we can obtain peace, self-acceptance, and release from the bondage of self-accusation. But the climactic moments of *God's* forgiveness described in scriptural accounts do not necessarily reflect the day-in-and-day-out experience of *self*-forgiveness. Even Alma and Paul speak ruefully of their past sins, suggesting that moments of sadness, shame, even grief over past failings can still recur after God has forgiven us and our repentance is complete. Certainly we can expect greater peace, more realistic self-assessments, more enduring hope than what we felt when we first faced our sinful state. But even doctrinal clarity, full repentance, and hard psychological labor will not always provide complete freedom from regret over past sins or shame about not overcoming current weaknesses.

More realistic goals for the habitually self-blaming might be:

+ that our self-recrimination become less severe, less easily triggered, less all-defining, and less unrelenting;
+ that we access more hope in the midst of our discouragement, more reassurance of our real worth despite periodic feelings of worthlessness;
+ that our trust in God's gentle mercy become a brighter beacon in the recurring darkness of the mortal journey;
+ that we see the temptation to despair about ourselves as just that, a temptation, rather than as a realistic response to who we truly are;
+ that we respond to that temptation with clear thinking, honest prayer, bids for support, realistic efforts to learn and grow, courageous acceptance of our limitations, and deeper trust in God's will and power to save us.

Not everyone will find permanent freedom from bouts of self-condemnation or anxiety about Judgment Day. We can, however, learn to talk back to our fears with sound doctrine and more balanced self-perspectives, rather than letting our fears take over without a fight. We can learn to more *grace-full-ly* adapt to life in the schism between our celestial ideals and our earthy limitations.

Such goals suggest a more modest miracle than our longed-for return to innocent sinlessness. But this is the miracle God seems to hold out as not just more realistic, but better. Given that evil, including our personal capacity for sin, is a permanent possibility in any world that includes human agency, God wants to teach us to deeply understand from personal experience both the value of the good so that we will desire and choose it, and the pain caused by evil so we will eschew it. Blind self-confidence and painless forgetting do not serve such ends. God's singular ability to bring good out of evil is not limited to eliminating evil from the world, or from our personal remembrance. Instead he allows us to know and remember the devastation caused by sin, then allows us to see and taste His ability to turn all things to our good if we will trust in the Atonement and allow our souls to be won by His love.

A NEW COVENANT

As a vital part of the new covenant God establishes with Israel in the last days, He promises that we can know the Lord—a promise of indescribable worth. How will this be accomplished? By having His law written in our hearts as we both learn to choose good over evil and experience being forgiven. Something about participating in this redemptive process seems to go straight to the soul to teach us about God's love—the essence of His character. This process is outlined in the following verses from Jeremiah:

Behold, the days come, saith the Lord, that I will make
a new covenant with the house of Israel, and with the house
of Judah. . . .

. . . I will put my law in their inward parts, and write it
in their hearts; and will be their God, and they shall be my
people.

And they shall teach no more every man his neigh-
bour, and every man his brother, saying, Know the Lord: for
they shall all know me, from the least of them unto the greatest of them, saith the Lord: *for I will forgive their iniquity, and
I will remember their sin no more* (Jeremiah 31:31, 33–34;
emphasis added).

As we learn by our own experience that God tells us the truth
and that competing versions of reality will fail us in the end, we
come to profoundly trust Him. We also trust His perfect plan for
His imperfect children. We begin to see more clearly who He really
is and gain hope that we too might acquire the charity and grace He
exemplifies. We comprehend that both the possibility of sin and the
offering of forgiveness are parts of the plan of mortality to which we
willingly submitted. We accept that regret and sorrow over our
sins and errors are part of the price we pay to participate in that plan.
We marvel at God's capacity to redeem—that is, to exchange things
of no worth (such as human weakness and sin) for things of great
value—learning, growth, wisdom, compassion, and ultimately exaltation—if we will trust in His will and power to save us. By receiving His forgiveness and grace, we begin to grasp the depth of His
goodness, the scope of His provisions, the magnitude of His love.

Even if the widow who fed Elijah fully understood the prophet's
message, she would have still been subject to hunger, sin, and loss.
But she might have also come to depend on another bottomless
barrel and cruse that are far more significant than those of grain or

oil. She might have reached with confidence for the bottomless barrel of God's love, the endless cruse of His mercy. Her son's death was apparently *not* a punishment for her past sin after all, but an opportunity for a prophet to demonstrate God's capacity to bring life out of even the most mortal moments. It can be so for us as well.

I have learned by experience that by submitting to the indignities of being human and mortal and then receiving the grace of Christ, we can come to not only know good from evil, but we can also know the Lord. Every loss, mistake, and humiliation of failure is worth this all-important end. The journey of amazing grace is the journey toward the loving face of God.

PART 1

CLARIFYING
OUR BELIEFS

Expecting and accepting God's mercy makes sense only if we understand the purposes of life and the place of sin and failure in God's plan. When we believe that God can and does forgive us, we can perhaps venture to forgive ourselves. Chapter 1 reviews key elements of the plan of salvation. Chapter 2 describes a model for understanding self-forgiveness and self-acceptance and their alternatives of delusion, despair, and distrust. Chapter 3 suggests ways that self-forgiveness blesses not only ourselves but others as well.

1

THE SPIRITUAL BASIS FOR SELF-FORGIVENESS

*Ever since the Fall God has been teaching men not
to fear, but with penitence to ask forgiveness in
full confidence of receiving it.*

—LDS BIBLE DICTIONARY[1]

Before reading this chapter, consider the following statements and mark each one true or false. If you think a statement is false, underline what is false.

1. Christ is the Only Begotten of the Father, the One whom God loves most.

2. Ideally, every one of us would be perfect during mortality, as Jesus Christ was.

3. If we cannot be perfect, our ultimate goal in life is to return to God in the same state of innocence and purity—as much as possible—we were in when we left Him.

4. If we do not obey God fully in all things, we will be in Satan's power.

5. Knowing that some of us would not pass the mortal test of obedience, God provided repentance as a backup plan for those who sin and fall short of their potential.

I will come back to these statements later, but I ask you about them here because I believe our assumptions about the plan of salvation deeply influence our receptivity to God's forgiveness. While we can gain a basic understanding of this plan by reading the scriptures or hearing the missionary lessons, even lifelong members of the Church can also misunderstand, mistrust, or misapply aspects of the plan in ways that undermine self-forgiveness.

Depression, anxiety, shame, or anger can distort one's understanding of gospel principles, even if the calm, rational self knows better. The fearful or shameful part of you may periodically hijack the mature, capable you that usually runs your life. This fearful part may have different ideas about God and His plan than the rest of you. As you look at the five statements above, carefully consider what this fearful part of you would say is true or false, versus what the rational self would say. These beliefs can powerfully affect self-forgiveness.

ALMA THE YOUNGER

Before we tackle the accuracy of the assumptions reflected in the true-false test, let's take a tour of a classic story of self-forgiveness—that of Alma the Younger in the Book of Mormon. Alma is an apostate who has been busily trying to destroy the Church; then he sees an angel who tells him he can destroy himself if he wants but to stop trying to destroy the Church of God. Alma is horrified to see and face the impact of his behavior. He falls into a comatose state for three days and nights, "harrowed up to the greatest degree and racked with all my sins." After months or years of telling himself his behavior was reasonable and appropriate, Alma says, "*I saw* that I had rebelled against my God," and he is "tormented with the pains of hell" (Alma 36:12–13; emphasis added). Perhaps we have our own version of this part of the story, the part where we finally *see* that we have been wrong, have hurt others or ourselves, or have rebelled against God.

A harrow is a farming instrument for turning over the soil, breaking it up and tearing it open so something new can grow there. Alma spends three long days being "harrowed up"—torn open by guilt and agony for his sins. He feels "inexpressible horror" at the very thought of facing God, a horror so complete that he wishes he could be "extinct both soul and body" (vv. 14–15). He contemplates his father's anguish, the damage to the Church, and the extent of his rebellion against God. Alma is "racked, even with the pains of a damned soul" (v. 16)—not because of some external punishment inflicted upon him by God but because he sees with horror his sin: he has allowed himself to be deceived and has ruined people's lives.

After three days of increasing, soul-wrenching clarity about his situation, the ground of Alma's soul has been thoroughly broken, "harrowed up," and prepared to receive the seed of faith. He has recalled and then "caught hold" of the teachings of his father about the Savior, and Alma calls upon Christ for deliverance. What can deliver people from the pain of seeing the harm they have done? Only the hope that it can be repaired. Alma cannot repair these damages, but the Spirit testifies with perfect clarity that Christ can. Christ can save not only Alma but also all those he has hurt. As Alma takes in the magnitude of the Atonement and the range of its reach, he is freed from his personal hell. His mind catches hold of the plan of redemption and the atonement of Christ, and he refuses to let go of the bright hope they inspire.

God has not sent us to this fallen world without making every provision to save us from it—if we will let Him. As Alma comprehends God's magnificent plan, he sees a vision of God upon His throne. Alma comes to know God—clearly, powerfully, personally. This happens, as described previously in Jeremiah 31:34, through receiving God's forgiveness. Alma's pain is swept away, and he is "harrowed up by the memory of [his] sins no more" (Alma 36:19, 22). This deliverance does not come because God doses him up with painkillers but because Alma grasps God's healing power to ensure that all our debts are paid when we repent. Alma's hopelessness about the pain he has caused can give way to hope.

There is a time for harrowing, but that time is *before*, not *after* the tender seeds of faith and repentance have begun to sprout. We need to not continue to harrow ourselves after we have changed our mind, heart, and behavior and glimpsed God's grace. We, like Alma, need to catch hold of God's saving plan and not let go.

THE PERFECT PLAN

The first step in the process of self-forgiveness is an accurate understanding of God's plan of agency, repentance, and Atonement. The LDS Bible Dictionary says repentance entails more than changed behavior. It also involves changing our *mind* or thoughts, acquiring a *fresh view*, and turning our *heart and will* to God.[2] Alma can begin to repent before he can even move because he acquires this fresh view, changes his mind, and turns his heart and will to God. He then spends the rest of his life living out that change of heart. He never forgets the debt he once owed—and undoubtedly he will always deeply regret the hurt he caused—but he can rejoice at God's perfect provision for all his debts to be paid.

REPENTANCE AND FAITH

How do we, like Alma, stop harrowing and start rejoicing?

We know from the fourth article of faith that the first principles of the gospel are faith in the Lord Jesus Christ and repentance. Self-forgiveness requires both. Changing our heart and behavior—repentance—is only one step toward self-forgiveness. Overcoming our doubts about God's will and power to save us "unworthy creatures" (Mosiah 4:11)—faith in Christ—is the other.

This plan was laid out in the beginning by our Heavenly Father. It gives us access to the rich but dangerous experiences of mortality with full assurance that we can still return to God. This plan required a perfect Redeemer to live a sinless life and then experience through the Atonement all the consequences of sin and mortality that we undergo here. In this way He could be our perfect Judge. He fully understands all our grievances against one another. He also fully understands the private pains out of which we injure one another. He fully empathizes with every one of us. In His omnipotence He is uniquely able to pay all our debts to one another, in part because there are no liens against Him.

Satan had, and still has, a different plan—one that requires each of us to be flawless so that no one would suffer at the hands of another. No one would have to feel pain or regret for sin because there would be no sinning. We would all be perfect in the sense of committing no wrongs. But in this plan we could never be perfect in the sense of being whole, complete, and like our Father—who is perfect because He fully understands all the options, none of which are closed to Him, and yet chooses good. There would have been no real need for a Savior in this plan, but Satan wanted the credit for coming up with this alternative plan. He wanted to be the Only Begotten, the beloved and sinless Firstborn. Sometimes we also long for that chosen status out of fear that we cannot *really* be loved by God unless we too are flawless.

In contrast, the Savior humbly offers to share with us all that He has. He acknowledges that we too have a difficult path to walk in mortality. He did His job so we could do ours. Because *I* struggle not to resent what others cost me or take comfort in my supposed superiority, I struggle to imagine a Christ who is neither resentful about what I have cost Him nor proud of His superiority. This plan requires humility from all who desire its full benefits.

I still remember a young woman who as a girl had been sexually violated by a family member. She still felt dirty and ashamed of this artifact of her life, and she longed to feel clean and pure like the good Latter-day Saint women around her. She had committed no sin at all, but she could not imagine any way to feel clean again short of going back in time and undoing the sin perpetrated against her. Whether it is the sin of someone else against us or the sin we have committed, the blood and sins of mortality seem to cling to us long after the moment of our wounding is past. Sometimes we believe that our purpose in mortality is to get back to God in a state as close as possible to the innocent, pure state we were in when we left Him. The more we become aware of the impossibility of accomplishing this, the more discouraged we become.

I am increasingly convinced that this is not the purpose of mortality at all. In fact, if this were our charge, our best course of action would be to lie down in our crib on the day we are born and never get up. What would be the point of God sending us here just to become such huge disappointments? No—we are here to do more than demonstrate our capacity for failure or to envy those who die before making a serious mistake. We are here to learn to be like our Father; to learn good from evil by our own experience; to learn to create, love, forgive, and bless; to learn the language of the Spirit; to progress and grow and develop; to exercise our agency to do good. These precious outcomes can be acquired only in a world of agency, challenge, and periodic failure.

We willingly chose to take that challenge, knowing that we would be eternally better off for coming here. We had nothing to lose and everything to gain. Some of us will make more of mortality than others, but all (except the sons of perdition) will be blessed by coming to earth, gaining a body, and stepping out of the crib of innocence and into the school of experience. While here we will both make and be subject to others making a lot of dumb choices. We will learn a lot of useless ideas, be subject to the deceiver, have a lot of human frailties, and commit a lot of sins. Still, we didn't cling to God's robes and beg Him not to send us here. We shouted for joy at the chance to come to earth and experience mortality, knowing we also had so much to gain.

We understood then what we don't see so clearly now: that God is a master, an expert, an absolute genius at turning trash into treasure, stupidity into wisdom, suffering into character, and sin (yes, even sin) into new life—*if*, and it is a big if—*if* we will let Him. *If* we will catch hold of the vision of His redeeming plan and not let go, *if* we will repent and have faith in the atonement of Christ, then God can not only save but also exalt us, even when we have been "the very vilest of sinners" (Mosiah 28:4).

As my daughter once taught me, "Repentance is not the backup plan; repentance *is* the plan." Repentance is not what is left after we have botched the true goal of obedience and undefiled righteousness. When learning from others' experience and failure has not been enough, repentance is a blessed part of how we *get to* obedience and undefiled righteousness—learning by our own experience and failure, trusting in God's love and sure provisions, activating our own reluctant resilience. This is the only path for us.

My culture taught me, "If a thing is worth doing it is worth doing well." I don't disagree. It is good to take the time to do better than a shoddy job. But another truth is sometimes even more applicable: "In order to do something well we must first be willing to do it badly."[3] Think about learning a language, a sport, a musical instrument; think about learning to run a meeting, care for a baby, drive a car; and then think about being a good home or visiting teacher, parenting a teenager, managing sexual temptation, overcoming addiction, discerning the Spirit, praying meaningfully. Things worth doing are worth doing imperfectly rather than throwing up our hands in defeat or sticking with what is easy and familiar. Doing the right things imperfectly, while we learn to do them better, is far more important than wasting time doing less important but easier things well. The best musicians learn to trust that the music they will ultimately make is more important than today's wrong notes.

Self-forgiveness requires a mature understanding of the purpose of life, which is *not* to get back to God in the same state of innocence and purity we were in when we left Him. Rather our charge here is to learn the compassion, humility, discipline, and understanding of good and evil that come only with experience and risk, failure and resilience. Our charge is to get back to God much, much wiser and better than when we left Him, something we can accomplish only through traveling the bruising, bloodying roads of mortal temptation, affliction, and periodic failure, as well as the roads of triumph, satisfaction, and ultimate joy.

LAB EXPERIMENTS AND
DRUM LESSONS

Two little stories have helped me imagine the hopeful picture the gospel lays out. I once heard a story, perhaps apocryphal, about Jonas Salk, the inventor of the vaccine that virtually ended polio in a single generation. Asked the secret of his genius, Salk credited his mother. He told of being a small boy eating cookies and milk at his mother's table and ignoring her warnings that his milk glass was too close to the edge of the table. Sure enough, his elbow caught the glass and the milk went flying. He noted that most parents would angrily point out that they had warned about this very possibility, but his mother took a different approach. She surveyed the situation and asked calmly, "Well, son, what have you learned?" He said that attitude allowed him to withstand the discouragement of a thousand failed experiments, learning from his errors instead of giving in to feelings of stupidity and futility.

Salk learned from his mother to face doing badly long enough to eventually do well. People who are skilled at appropriate self-forgiveness cultivate a similar learning focus.

The second story is more an explanation of two different ways to look at the world: the Western way, which developed out of Greek thought, and the Eastern way familiar to the ancient Hebrews. James E. Faulconer explains:

> We think of the past as gone forever ... [so] the passing of time becomes a difficult problem for Western thinkers. The problem is especially acute for Christians, for if the past is gone once and for all, redemption and atonement are incomprehensible. The Greek Christian may think, "I have sinned. Nothing can change that, and any recompense, whether by me or by God himself, is a poor substitute for

what should have happened in the first place." In the Western mind, history is a series of nows that disappear forever, and, once gone, they cannot be changed or redone. The form of events is fixed forever by the passing of time.

In contrast, if we conceive time rhythmically, as the Hebrews do, then the past can change. The previous moment of the rhythm still occurred, but the past exists and has its meaning only in relation to the continuation of the rhythm, only in relation to the present and future of the rhythm. As I noted earlier, the relation of one drum beat to the previous and subsequent beats determines the rhythmic meaning of any beat of a drum. Thus a present beat determines the rhythmic meaning of a past beat as much as the beats that came before determine the rhythmic meaning of a present beat. In rhythm, causation runs backward as well as forward.[4]

If God lives in an eternal now where time is cyclical and rhythmic, not static and linear as we see it, then turning back the clock is not the only way to make things right again. The drum beat of sin that occurred yesterday still exists, but its meaning is changed by the rhythm of learning and repentance created by subsequent beats. We don't get to God by turning the clock back to reclaim the lost innocence of Eden. We get to God by going forward through a sometimes dreary but astounding world of learning and discovery. We are not here to be quiet, but to learn to make the beautiful music of endless creativity and life.

IT ISN'T THE HEAT, IT'S THE . . .

So we all sin, and we all are subject to the burning heat of shame and guilt. We quickly learn in humid climates that temperature alone does not control how hot we feel. In a similar way, it is almost never our sin or failure itself that does us in; we are done in by what we tell ourselves the failure means about us. While we cannot undo the sin, fortunately we *can* change what we tell ourselves that sin means about us. Inaccurate beliefs are in our control, and they are often the real source of our depression and excessive shame.

For example, Peggy did not pay her tithing when her children were young, and although she pays it now she believes her children's financial irresponsibility goes back to her early choices. She tells herself that because of her mistake:

- "God will never accept me now."
- "I can never be as good as others."
- "I can never really change the damage already done."
- "I do not deserve to be happy."
- "Everyone who finds out will dislike me."
- "My children are doomed to have problems."
- "I have lost my right to promised blessings."

While Peggy cannot change the past, she can make sure she is not fettered with hopelessness because of erroneous beliefs. Such beliefs obscure our strengths, virtues, and righteous desires. They reduce us to our problems. They encourage us to see temporary weaknesses as more important than enduring strengths. They deny the power of God to save and change us.

I wrote earlier of a young woman who had been sexually violated. Like Peggy, she cannot change the past, as much as some part of her wants desperately to believe that if she is angry and inconsolable enough, then perhaps this tragedy will somehow dematerialize. But she can change what she believes the past means about her. To be sure, she will also have to grieve the loss of her innocent trust in other people and make peace with her own capacity for hatred—terrible prices to have to pay for someone else's selfish sin. But she does not have to add to her burden the beliefs that:

+ "I was not worth protecting."
+ "No good person will want me."
+ "I must have done something to deserve this."
+ "I can never be truly happy again."

How do we change these distorted beliefs? First, we identify them for what they are. When you struggle, what are you likely to tell yourself or to believe? Think about a recent time when you doubted your worth or wrestled with self-condemnation. Chances are good that your thoughts included ideas like those on the two lists above. Check any of the above that are familiar to you and add others you are aware of.

Self-hateful feelings follow quite naturally from such thoughts. If I really believe—and in that moment I do—that I am eternally unacceptable to God, inherently worse than other people, incapable of improvement, undeserving of happiness because of the depth of my evil, unlikable, unfit to parent, and lost to all goodness, it is easy to see why I won't feel very good about myself (if I'm a good person, that is; ironically, if I'm really hopelessly evil I won't care about any of this). Unfortunately, some of us don't stop to think about whether these thoughts are true. We don't even really think about what we are thinking at all. We just start to feel awful about ourselves and assume those feelings are legitimate and flow from our *irreversible* behavior or past, not from our *reversible* thoughts about what our behavior or experience means about us. We don't realize that we control the next beat of the drum, but instead we incessantly beat out: "I'm scum! I'm scum! I'm scum!"

But such thoughts are full of distortions; if we really understand the plan of salvation, we do not have to follow the drum beat of sin. Even if we have been warned about our potential for spilling milk, we are still asked by a loving Father what we have learned, not condemned as hopelessly incompetent for our clumsiness. While we, like Alma, may have sinned, even in terrible ways, we are not automatically cast off without hope. Even the most heinous of our sins or others' crimes do not put us outside the reach of God's will and power to save us.

How would you rewrite the statements above? Try your hand at seeing the all-or-nothing thinking in these statements and rewriting them to more accurately reflect promises and teachings of the scriptures.

- "God will never accept me now that I've made such a big mistake."
- Your rewrite (see Genesis 4:6–7):

_____

- "I can never be as good as others."
- Your rewrite (see 2 Nephi 26:24–28):

_____

- "I can never really change."
- Your rewrite (see 2 Nephi 2:26–29):

_____

- "I do not deserve to be happy."
- Your rewrite (see Alma 36:5, 6, 21):

_____

- "Others will not like me if they find out."
- Your rewrite (see Ether 12:25–28):

_____

- "My children are doomed."
- Your rewrite (see Moses 6:54):

_____

+ "I have lost my right to promised blessings."
+ Your rewrite (see Isaiah 1:16–19):

_____

+ "I was not worth protecting."
+ Your rewrite (see Alma 14:10–11):

_____

+ "No good person will want me."
+ Your rewrite (see Matthew 18:10–14):

_____

+ "I must have done something to deserve this."
+ Your rewrite (see JST Matthew 18:6–9):

_____

+ "I can never be truly happy again."
+ Your rewrite (see Revelation 7:13–17):

_____

+ Other common thoughts of yours (fill in the blanks):

_____

_____

_____

+ Your rewrite (fill in the blank):

_____

If you struggle to rewrite any of these, look up the scriptures or ask someone else how they would rewrite them. In moments of self-recrimination, watch for inaccurate beliefs that might affect your self-judgment. Write them down, rewrite them for accuracy, and tell yourself the truth.

THREE LIES AND A TRUTH

It is fun to play the parlor game in which players make up three outlandish things about themselves, throw in one thing that is true, and has everyone guess which is which. But it is not so fun to play with truth and lies in real life. Lies hurt, and the biggest lies and the biggest hurts come from the Biggest Deceiver. He lies about sin, convincing us that it is not all that bad—or that it places us beyond redemption. He lies about life, telling us that we deserve to feel perfect and safe, something *he* can accomplish only through encouraging our defenses, addictions, and denials. He lies about God, telling us that God can be ignored at will—or that He is an angry, never-satisfied taskmaster.

Going back to the statements at the beginning of this chapter, what is true and what is a lie?

1. Christ is the Only Begotten of the Father, the One God loves most.

While Christ is the Only Begotten, He is not the Only Beloved. We do not have to be as perfect as Christ to merit God's love and concern. In fact, it is because God loves *us*, each of us individually, that He provided a plan for *our* growth, learning, and eventual redemption through Christ's atonement. He did not plan to exalt only Christ; He also planned to exalt as many of us as will let Him. Christ did His job so we can do ours without fear that the risks of mortality are too dangerous to take.

2. Ideally, every one of us would be perfect during mortality, as Jesus Christ was.

While this sounds good on the surface, this is actually Satan's plan. God knew, and we knew, there would be only one Perfect One. The rest of us would accomplish our missions by learning from experience as both agents and targets of good and evil. We attain perfection through experience with imperfection, "relying wholly upon the merits of him who is mighty to save" (2 Nephi 31:19).

3. Since we cannot be perfect, our ultimate goal in life is to return to God in the same state of innocence and purity we were in—as much as possible—when we left Him.

While righteous living and faithful obedience are always our goals, the tasks of learning to create, love, serve, parent, lead, follow, obey, choose, and become more like God are so important that they are worth doing imperfectly as we learn to do them well. We are better off taking the risks of trying these things than not attempting them for fear of making a mistake. Mortality is a series of tests, but tests we can keep retaking until we get them right. There may be serious, even lasting consequences for our poor choices, but God promises that "as often as my people repent will I forgive them" (Mosiah 26:30).

4. If we do not obey God fully in all things, we will be in Satan's power.

Satan would like us to believe this because it leads us to hopelessness and despair. In fact, this statement would be true *except* for the one crucial, all-important fact of the atonement of Jesus Christ. This is why the Atonement means the difference between life and death, hope and despair, God's plan and Satan's plan. The atonement of Christ is the most important event ever to happen on this earth because it alone turns the gift of agency from an inevitable death sentence into a vehicle toward life and exaltation. The best response to this threat from Satan is to cast it from us.

5. Knowing that some of us would not pass the mortal test of obedience, God provided repentance as a backup plan for those who sin and fall short of their potential.

Repentance is not a backup plan; *repentance is the plan* for every one of us. It is not just the plan for sinners, any more than it is just the plan for the righteous (which we also are tempted to believe). We all have the capacity for both sin and righteousness. We need not feel ashamed of our need to repent.

Just as Christ offers us the perfect example of how to live well, Adam and Eve show us the perfect example of how to repent: taking responsibility for their actions, submitting to the consequences of their choices, learning from their mistakes, and trusting fully in God's ability to bring good out of their transgression as they covenant with Him. Perhaps that is why the story of imperfect but repentant Adam and Eve is highlighted in the ordinances of the temple.

Amid Satan's lies, God tells us this one perfect truth: He knows how to redeem us, and being redeemed is even better for us than being flawless but without experience. God tells us plainly that it will be hard and lonely here; that we will not be protected from struggle, loss, the sins of others, or personal failure; and that Christ is the Great Redeemer—not the Great Preventer. Still, God promises that the plan of agency, error, and redemption is worth both pain and failure. He further promises that He has the will and the power to save us through the atonement of Christ. Choosing to trust God's forgiveness once we have repented is a choice to humbly trust God and His plan over Satan's lies—not a choice to be lenient with ourselves.

The path toward grace and self-forgiveness starts here—with understanding that God's plan is based on the expectation that each of us will be mortal, fallible, fallen. While He offers us the privilege of living His laws and rejoices when we do, He understands that learning to cherish what He cherishes takes experience. While He is delighted when we avoid sin and saddened by the harm that sinful behavior causes, He judges us less by the number of our misdeeds than by the depth of our repentance. We can trust Him to always be close at hand, gently whispering, "What did you learn?"

2

DEFINING
SELF-FORGIVENESS

*Behold, ye are little children and ye cannot bear all things
now; ye must grow in grace and in the knowledge of the
truth. Fear not, little children, for you are mine, and I
have overcome the world, and you are of them that
my Father hath given me; and none of them that my
Father hath given me shall be lost.*

—DOCTRINE AND COVENANTS 50:40–42

A good working definition of self-forgiveness might be "trusting
that God's gift of forgiveness applies to my sins and mistakes." For
faithful Christians, self-forgiveness is neither meaningful nor possible without God's forgiveness. God is uniquely positioned to
understand the circumstances affecting our choices and the sincerity of our repentance, making His forgiveness prerequisite to our
own.

God's forgiveness is an abstract concept until we determine that
it applies to us. We may trust God's power to forgive in general,

but we may believe (rightly or wrongly) that we have not done enough to warrant forgiveness or that our heart is not right despite our appropriate behavior. We may feel hopeless about our capacity to change or believe we are too inherently bad to be forgiven. We may believe that God is too disappointed in us to completely forgive us. We may think we trust in God's forgiveness, but our self-talk is filled with so much self-blame that we think we know more than God about what is fair or true, and that we trust our own opinions about ourselves more than His. In contrast, we may sin without acknowledging it and so not repent or seek forgiveness at all. All of these positions put us outside of the scope of genuine and appropriate self-forgiveness.

GOD'S PROMISED GIFT

Does God really mean it when He promises the gift of forgiveness? Is it okay to forgive ourselves? Can we afford to trust that even our most terrible sins are within His reach? As just a sampling from each of the standard works, consider the following:

Come now, and let us reason together, saith the Lord: though your sins be as scarlet, they shall be as white as snow; though they be red like crimson, they shall be as wool (Isaiah 1:18).

For I will be merciful to their unrighteousness, and their sins and their iniquities will I remember no more (Hebrews 8:12).

But as oft as they repented and sought forgiveness, with real intent, they were forgiven (Moroni 6:8).

Behold, he who has repented of his sins, the same is forgiven, and I, the Lord, remember them no more (D&C 58:42).

And finally, here is one of the most powerful statements anywhere on the consummate power of the Atonement, from President Boyd K. Packer at the November 1995 general conference of the Church:

Restoring what you cannot restore, healing the wound you cannot heal, fixing that which you broke and cannot fix is the very purpose of the atonement of Christ.

When your desire is firm and you are willing to pay the "uttermost farthing" (see Matt. 5:25–26), the law of restitution is suspended. Your obligation is transferred to the Lord. He will settle your accounts.

I repeat, save for the exception of the very few who defect to perdition, there is no habit, no addiction, no rebellion, no transgression, no apostasy, no crime exempted from the promise of complete forgiveness. This is the promise of the atonement of Christ.[1]

God's promise is clear and oft repeated: when we repent, He forgives.

INSUFFICIENT SELF-BLAME

While some struggle to claim the forgiveness God offers, others let themselves off the hook too easily. They may not have really developed their capacity for empathy with the pain of others, or they may harbor deep doubts about their ability to really change. Other people have difficulty acknowledging errors because their shaky self-esteem depends on being faultless or superior. They may naively expect everything to return to normal before they have grasped the seriousness of the injury they've caused, made appropriate restitution and apology, truly changed, and given the injured parties time to heal. This cheap self-forgiveness takes a big toll, however, on both relationships and self-esteem. People in this category might include:

- A spouse who stews in anger and blame after a disagreement because acknowledging her own part of the problem makes her feel childish and small
- An overburdened bishop who brushes off a ward member he has hurt because his fragile self-esteem cannot tolerate yet one more criticism or demand
- A teenager who angrily accuses her parents of excessive strictness and withdraws into drugs rather than face her fears about succeeding as a responsible grown-up
- An adulterous husband who harps on his adult children for not forgiving him rather than face the extent of the devastation he has caused
- A home teacher who quits home teaching but always reports it as done, laughing about how silly the home teaching program is anyway

These situations call for both deeper understanding of our real worth in the eyes of God and deeper repentance. Trusting God and turning our hearts to Him take courage. Cheap self-forgiveness is an inadequate substitute for real repentance and reliance on the Atonement.

EXCESSIVE SELF-BLAME

Given the problems with cheap forgiveness, is stoking the fire of self-blame really a problem? Isn't it better to overdo guilt than underdo it? After all, if we feel deeply ashamed about our sins, won't we be less likely to repeat them?

Not necessarily. Excessive self-blame is as problematic as insufficient self-blame because excessive self-blame tempts us to give up on ourselves. It reduces us to the lowest common denominator of our most despicable moments. It makes us lose our sense of other people, seeing them only as our competitors for the Good Person prize. It distorts our view of God, who becomes the Great Ruthless Judge in the Sky waiting for the worst possible moment to shame and punish us if we stop our self-reprisals. Our misperceptions thwart our self-esteem, damage our loving relationships, and undermine our trust in the one Person we can count on to always tell us the truth.

THE MIDDLE PATH

Somewhere between ignoring responsibility for our sins and excessive self-castigation lies the path of self-forgiveness and self-acceptance. Self-forgiveness and self-acceptance are different, however. Self-forgiveness means we acknowledge we have sinned and have tried to change. It is not just about being nice to ourselves; it also requires being true to ourselves. When we injure other people by our selfishness, violate our moral standards, break the law or the commandments, or lie to God about our true allegiance, we have to change to merit forgiveness.

Self-acceptance, by contrast, means accepting that we have real limits on our wisdom, judgment, energy, and foresight. We cannot change or remove all human weakness. Weakness is given to us by God to call us to humility, learning, and patience. We can overcome sin through the about-face of repentance, but we will not overcome all our weaknesses in this life.

We can fail ourselves or others out of either sin or weakness. The distinction between the two is very important because sin and weakness have entirely different authors, call for somewhat different courses of action, and lead to different outcomes. Let's look more closely at these differences.

SIN, REPENTANCE, AND FORGIVENESS

Sin is described in the scriptures as willful disobedience or rebellion. Sins are intentional violations of the laws of God and include anything we do to rebel against God, ignore His commandments, believe Satan or other people more than God, or intentionally hurt innocent people. Sin is the most dangerous state for us to be in because it stops our progress and leads to misery. When we use our agency to continue in sin, we make a big statement about who we are and what we love. Because sin is by definition rebellion against God, no sin is trivial.

Satan is the author of sin, and he makes sin look enticing and inevitable. No one who fully understands God's wisdom and goodness would deliberately choose Satan's paths over God's paths, so we have to deceive ourselves to go along with sin. We convince ourselves that God doesn't quite know what He is talking about, or that what we are choosing really *is* God's will even though it isn't consistent with His commandments, or that there is no God at all. We all sin at various points in life, as Paul affirms to the Romans: "For all have sinned, and come short of the glory of God" (Romans 3:23). Unrepentant sinners place themselves beyond God's saving power. Even otherwise good people sin, justify their behavior, and fail to repent.

Most sin results from pride—thinking we know more or are better than other people. Our pride can become hubris—thinking we know more than God (even though we don't think of it that way at the time). This is why sin is equated with idolatry—the worship of anything other than God. The clear scriptural mandate for sin is repentance, which means turning our heart and will to God, worshiping only Him, and realigning our lives with His teachings. Repentance requires:

+ Acknowledgment of sin
+ Sincere apology to those we've injured
+ Restitution so far as possible for the damage we did
+ Renewed worship of and trust in God alone
+ Obedience to God's commandments

The scriptures assure us that once we repent God will forgive us. This promise is sure. Forgiveness is described as canceling the debt we owe (Matthew 6:12; Luke 7:42), cleansing us from the stain of sin (Isaiah 1:18; Jeremiah 33:8), releasing us from hell (Psalm 86:13; D&C 138:58–59), and stopping further punishment (Ezra 9:13; D&C 19:20)—although not necessarily rescinding natural consequences of our choices (compare Moses 6:53 and Moses 4:29–31). The atonement Christ made gives Him the right to forgive our sin on condition of our repentance.

WEAKNESS, HUMILITY, AND GRACE

Sin is not the only expression of human failure, however. Human weakness is also responsible. Weakness, inherent in the mortal condition, includes limitations on endurance, judgment, wisdom, energy, skill, resilience, or physical capacity. Human weakness sets us up to fail at important tasks because we lack experience, training, or understanding. Human weakness means we will hurt other people out of ignorance, misunderstanding, or insecurity.

Weakness includes susceptibility to disease, emotional disorders, temptations, same-gender attractions, addictions, and death. Because of our inherent weakness we may be awkward, unskilled, immature, or handicapped in a variety of ways. Such human emotions as anger, worry, fear, sadness, and pleasure are also inherently weak when untutored.

Weakness can lead to sin, but weakness in itself is not sin. In fact, God is the author of human weakness, while Satan is the author of sin. We are weak by design, as part of the mortal experience. God is patient and tolerant with human weakness, yet He cannot look upon sin with the least degree of allowance.

Rather than induce sinful pride, awareness of our weakness generally induces shame about how poorly we compare with other people. But many scriptures suggest that the appropriate response to weakness is the opposite of shame: genuine humility. In the book of Ether, the Lord gives a succinct explanation of the relationship among weakness, humility, and grace. He says:

> And if men come unto me I will show unto them their weakness. I give unto men weakness that they may be humble; and my grace is sufficient for all men that humble themselves before me; for if they humble themselves before me, and have faith in me, then will I make weak things become strong unto them (Ether 12:27).

We are to come to God and prayerfully ask Him to show us our weakness. We are then to humble ourselves and seek God's grace. Humility overlaps somewhat with repentance but also differs in important ways. Humility includes:

- Acknowledgment of our limitations and errors
- Sincere apology for the harm we cause

- Willingness to learn and improve
- Prioritizing our goals because we cannot do everything at once
- Developing our strengths as well as reducing our shortcomings
- Practice and patience

Both repentance for sin and humility for weakness call us to acknowledge our faults and apologize, but sin requires us to do an about-face and return to God, while weakness calls for gradual improvement as we learn and grow. In our weakness we cannot do everything at once. We may need to experiment with different options, practice and improve over time, build on our strengths, actively try even though we don't always succeed, and learn from our errors. But we can be weak and still have our heart in the right place with God.

Once we respond to our weakness with humility, God offers us His grace. Most of us are familiar with Nephi's teaching that "it is by grace that we are saved, after all we can do" (2 Nephi 25:23). Just as charity is a special word for Christ's love for us—love we cannot fully understand without spiritual help—grace is a special word for God's particular brand of goodness to us, also beyond our full understanding. The LDS Bible Dictionary defines grace as "help or strength, given through the bounteous mercy and love of Jesus Christ."[2]

In the same way that God offers forgiveness to the penitent sinner, He offers grace to the weak but humble. Forgiveness is akin to cleansing, freeing, or canceling a debt, while grace refers to divine help or strength. The Bible Dictionary further explains, "Divine grace is needed by every soul in consequence of the fall of Adam and also because of man's weaknesses and shortcomings." Grace is "an enabling power" by which weak humans may "receive strength and assistance to do good works that they otherwise would not be able to maintain if left to their own means."[3] Forgiveness helps us overcome the effects of sin; grace helps us to do good despite our human weakness.

Elder Dallin H. Oaks distinguishes sin from mistakes, which are one type of weakness. He writes:

> Sins result from willful disobedience of laws we have received by explicit teaching or by the Spirit of Christ, which teaches every man the general principles of right and wrong. For sins, the remedy is to chasten and encourage repentance.
>
> Mistakes result from ignorance of the laws of God or the workings of the universe or people he has created. For mistakes, the remedy is to correct the mistake, not to condemn the individual.
>
> We must make every effort to avoid sin and to repent when we fall short. Through the Atonement of Jesus Christ we can be forgiven of our sins through repentance and baptism and by earnestly striving to keep the commandments of God. . . .
>
> We should seek to avoid mistakes, since some mistakes have very painful consequences. But we do not seek to avoid mistakes at all costs. Mistakes are inevitable in the process of growth in mortality. To avoid all possibility of error is to avoid all possibility of growth.[4]

God reproves us when we sin but comforts, relieves, and helps us in our weakness. This is also possible because of the atonement of Christ. Through Christ's atonement He took upon Himself our weaknesses, including our pains, afflictions, temptations, sicknesses, death, and infirmities, "that his bowels may be filled with mercy, according to the flesh, that he may know according to the flesh how to succor his people according to their infirmities" (Alma 7:11–12). Christ also took "upon him the sins of his people, that he might blot out their transgressions according to the power of his deliverance" (v. 13). Because of His atonement He can both succor us in our weakness and blot out our sins when we repent.

SIN VERSUS WEAKNESS

Knowing whether repentance and self-forgiveness or humility and self-acceptance are called for is not always straightforward. Sometimes we need more repentance, eyes that see our self-deception, renewed obedience, and faith in Christ's redemption; we then need to apologize, accept responsibility, and change. Other times we need more humility about our weakness, inexperience, limitations, and mistakes; we then need to stop comparing ourselves to others, humbly try to improve, and trust that God's grace is sufficient. These are not easy distinctions to make, however, and most of us struggle to see ourselves accurately. Claiming we are weak when in fact we are sinful leads to dangerous self-justification for sin. Claiming we are sinful when in fact we are weak leads to dangerous despair and hopelessness. If we don't recognize our sin for what it is, we don't repent and obtain forgiveness (cleansing from stain and canceling of our debts). If we don't recognize our weakness for what it is, we don't humble ourselves to obtain grace (help, support, and comfort). The Spirit of God and often the counsel of others are essential in helping us make these distinctions.

Consider the calling of Moses as a prophet in Exodus 3 and 4. When called to lead Israel, Moses first points out his human weakness: worry about his lack of leadership stature, fear of Pharaoh and of the Jews, inadequacy in public speaking. God patiently responds to each concern with promises of grace: help, words of encouragement, miracles to perform, and answers to questions. God's grace is sufficient for Moses's human weakness. But then, in a plea arising from "human weakness," Moses asks God to get someone else for the job. God becomes angry with Moses, indicating that this request reflects not weakness but the sin of distrusting God and disobeying a divine call. Moses appropriately responds with repentance and obedience.

From this example we see that weakness and sin differ but coincide. What I think of as weakness—suggesting I need help, comfort, support, and acceptance—someone else may believe is sin for which they expect me to change my heart, apologize, make restitution, and reform. We need our own careful reasoning, the help of other people, and the inspiration of the Holy Ghost to distinguish sin and weakness. Our intentions and desires can be more important than our behavior in making this distinction. Both sin and weakness can seriously harm other people, distance us from God, and evoke guilt. Both call for humility and efforts to change and improve. But sin also requires us to repent, which includes rejecting our behavior and turning our heart and will back to God, while weakness requires accepting our mortal condition and trusting God's grace despite our limitations.

Some examples from the standard works of the role of grace in coping with weakness include:

> And he [God] said unto me [Paul], My grace is sufficient for thee: for my strength is made perfect in weakness. Most gladly therefore will I rather glory in my infirmities, that the power of Christ may rest upon me.
>
> Therefore I take pleasure in infirmities, in reproaches, in necessities, in persecutions, in distresses for Christ's sake: for when I am weak, then am I strong (2 Corinthians 12:9–10).

For we have not an high priest which cannot be touched with the feeling of our infirmities; but was in all points tempted like as we are, yet without sin.

Let us therefore come boldly unto the throne of grace, that we may obtain mercy, and find grace to help in time of need (Hebrews 4:15–16).

Nevertheless, the Lord God showeth us our weakness that we may know that it is by his grace, and his great condescensions unto the children of men, that we have power ... (Jacob 4:7).

Behold, and hearken, O ye elders of my church, saith the Lord your God, even Jesus Christ, your advocate, who knoweth the weakness of man and how to succor them who are tempted (D&C 62:1).

As a more current example of how sin and weakness interplay in our lives, let's look at a tired mother who is short-tempered with her children. They are at the grocery store at the end of a long day, and the kids are wound up and demanding. The mother is embarrassed by the disapproving looks of other shoppers. After some effort to bribe or cajole the kids into behaving, she starts yelling, threatening, and spanking them. When they cry she abandons the shopping basket and marches them to the car without speaking to them. At home she sends them to their bedrooms without dinner, and the evening disintegrates into tantrums and tears.

This young mother clearly has mortal weakness and limitations working against her. She is battling a weary body, overloaded emotions, inexperience with child-rearing, limited knowledge of her options, lack of support and mentoring from skilled others, and shame about her inadequacies. The appropriate response to such weakness is humility, pleas for God's help, apologies to her children, and renewed efforts to develop patience and parenting skill. But is her behavior also sinful? Certainly she does not look very loving, patient, kind, wise, or godly in her treatment of her children, but is she deliberately disobedient, rebellious, or disbelieving? We probably cannot know from just a description of her behavior. She may be doing pretty much the best she can, or she may have made choices that constitute—for her—rebellion and deliberate disobedience, such as neglecting to pray, ignoring spiritual promptings, refusing help out of pride, or deliberately choosing to put herself in the path of temptation to anger. Asking for others' counsel, studying the scriptures, and praying for discernment may help her know which of her misdeeds call for more humility and grace and which require repentance.

Other situations in which sin and weakness may both play a role are addictions, same-gender attractions, emotional disorders, inactivity in the Church, relationship difficulties, work problems, and many other complex human experiences. We may also benefit from considering the relative roles of sin and weakness in omissions like failing to pray, read scriptures, attend the temple, or teach our children the gospel. Sin requires an about-face, a change of heart and behavior; weakness requires learning, persistence, prioritizing, and focus on our strengths.

A MODEL

Our inner voices, the frustration of people we care about, the unpleasant consequences of our poor choices, the whispering of the Holy Ghost—any of these may prompt us to take a hard look at both our basic nature ("Am I a good person?") and our specific choices ("Did I do the right thing?"). Depending on our answers to these questions and our subsequent choices, we can move toward self-forgiveness or self-acceptance, or we can get stuck in delusion, despair, or distrust of God.

Consider two diagrams that illustrate these concepts. Diagram 1 assumes that we have committed a sin, and Diagram 2 (page 44) assumes that we have a mortal weakness. On the left side of each diagram we'll put our self-assessment—how we judge ourselves and our behavior. For simplicity, we'll say we can either find ourselves and our behavior acceptable or unacceptable, although of course there is a wide range in between. In Diagram 1 we are dealing with sin, for which the appropriate response is repentance, represented by the bottom axis. Repentance includes rejection of sin, change of heart and behavior, apology, and restitution.

	POSITIVE	Delusion	Self-Forgiveness
SELF-ASSESSMENT	NEGATIVE	Despair	Distrust
		UNREPENTANT	REPENTANT
		EXTENT OF REPENTANCE	

Diagram 1: Responses to Sin

Depending on our self-assessment and level of repentance, we can end up in one of four places. At the top left is Delusion, which is what happens when we have sinned but do not acknowledge it and do not repent. We fool ourselves into thinking that our behavior is justified. We do not obtain God's forgiveness because we do not seek it or qualify for it. In order to move toward genuine self-forgiveness, people in this box may need more awareness of the problems created by their sinful behavior, more clarity about God's commandments, or more confidence in the possibility of change.

On the bottom left is Despair, which is what happens when we judge ourselves negatively but don't repent. Often people in this box dislike themselves and their behavior but have given up hope of change. To move toward Self-Forgiveness, they need more hope that change is possible, more courage to tackle their difficulties, and more trust in the atonement of Christ.

On the bottom right is Distrust. People in this quadrant change their behavior and have righteous desires, but they mistakenly think they can never do enough to merit forgiveness. They may erroneously believe they have a fatal flaw that nullifies repentance or blocks forgiveness. They have been forgiven by God because they have repented, but they don't forgive themselves, not trusting that God's forgiveness applies to them personally. They need greater clarity about God's plan, more empathy for themselves, better understanding of the difference between sin and weakness, and help managing recurrent feelings of shame and guilt.

On the top right is Self-Forgiveness, which is trust that God's gift of forgiveness applies to our sin. In this quadrant people can both like themselves and dislike past choices they have made. They can accept that they have sinned without losing hope. They do all they can to change their heart and behavior, apologize, and make restitution for their sin. They accept God's forgiveness as a precious gift to be received with deep gratitude.

Diagram 2 (see next page) suggests what happens when we deal with mortal weakness rather than sin. At the bottom of Diagram 2 is humility and growth through acceptance of weakness, learning, prioritizing, and practicing. Humility is the appropriate response when facing our limitations and weakness.

SELF-ASSESSMENT	**POSITIVE**	Delusion	Self-Acceptance
	NEGATIVE	Despair	Distrust
		No Growth	Much Growth
		HUMILITY	

Diagram 2: Responses to Weakness

Because Delusion, Despair, and Distrust often stem from enduring personality styles and conclusions drawn from our early experiences, they show up in response to mortal weakness as they do in response to sin. The top left quadrant of Delusion, people fail to humble themselves, learn from their weakness, and make the effort to improve because they deny being weak or that their weakness is consequential. The bottom left quadrant of Despair is characterized by a lack of pride: the person recognizes his or her faults but experiences shame-based humiliation rather than true humility. People may choose this quadrant because they unconsciously believe they get benefit from staying in a one-down position. In the bottom right quadrant of Distrust, people may work hard to learn and improve but fail to take needed risks for fear that God will not help them. In the top right quadrant of Self-Acceptance, people are able to like themselves despite mortal limitations, secure in the promise that learning and growth are possible through God's grace.

People in both Diagram 1 and Diagram 2 often have deeply held beliefs that keep them stuck and prevent them from moving toward self-forgiveness and self-acceptance. Part 3 of this book examines the personality styles and beliefs associated with each of these quadrants, helping us see our need for healing, insight, or a change of mind to move us toward greater self-forgiveness and self-acceptance.

MANIFESTATIONS OF SELF-FORGIVENESS AND SELF-ACCEPTANCE

We can measure the degree of self-forgiveness and self-acceptance we allow by noticing how we talk to ourselves about our sin and weakness. Self-talk focused on fear of being exposed, anger and disgust with ourselves, longing for return to innocence, or punishment we deserve suggests that we have some work to do to move out of Distrust or Despair and toward Self-Forgiveness. Our negative self-talk may reflect beliefs common to our particular personality or experience. We can learn to refute or ignore our negative self-talk and increase our genuine empathy and compassion for ourselves. The remainder of this book will attempt to expose and help us countermand self-talk that interferes with self-compassion and self-forgiveness.

Satan will tempt us to abandon hope in the modest virtues of self-forgiveness and self-acceptance. He will strive to weaken our trust in the Atonement. God tells us the truth about the Atonement's power to cleanse, heal, and empower, and Satan tells us something else. Satan's lies will fail us in the end, leaving us wandering in dark mists of delusion, despair, and distrust. Repentance and humility place us squarely on the strait and narrow path of God's life-giving love.

3

RECEIVING THE GIFT

For what doth it profit a man if a gift is bestowed upon him, and he receive not the gift? Behold, he rejoices not in that which is given unto him, neither rejoices in him who is the giver of the gift.

—Doctrine and Covenants 88:33

I am so grateful for the Book of Mormon story of Alma's sins and subsequent repentance. But imagine if Alma had recounted his sins, his angelic visit, his three days of torment over his sins, and then ended, "and after that I just never could forgive myself." Consider how different the message of the Book of Mormon would be if King Lamoni had said, after hearing Ammon teach about Jesus Christ and the need for repentance, "I hear what you're saying, but I've killed too many people to ever hope for mercy." Or if Nephi, after lamenting, "O wretched man that I am! Yea, my heart sorroweth because of my flesh; my soul grieveth because of mine iniquities. I am encompassed about, because of the temptations and the sins which do so easily beset me," had never gotten to "nevertheless, I know in whom I have trusted. . . . O Lord, I have trusted in thee, and I will trust in thee forever" (2 Nephi 4:17, 18, 34).

These individuals regretted their past sins and struggled to surmount them, but their soul-filled acceptance of the atonement of Christ constitutes more than God's gift to them. Their trust in God is also a gift to us—a gift of hope, example, courage, and resilience. When we fully receive God's forgiveness and achieve true self-forgiveness, others also benefit.

SELF-FORGIVENESS CAN BENEFIT OTHERS

When we encourage others to forgive we will often say, "Forgiving others is really a gift you give yourself." The same principle applies in reverse to self-forgiveness. It is not just something to help us feel better; rather, forgiving ourselves after sincere repentance is also a gift to those we love. It shows others what it means to be both a fallen mortal and a faithful believer. Let's take a deeper look at the blessings others receive when we appropriately forgive ourselves.

Modeling self-forgiveness. Modeling self-forgiveness sets an example for those we love so they will know they can forgive themselves too. Even if we think we need self-blame to keep ourselves in line, most of us would not wish upon our children an internal voice of self-hatred constantly berating them for their failures. People we love can learn about self-forgiveness by seeing us take responsibility for our errors, make sincere apologies and changes, and then let go. They benefit from hearing us say, "I feel so bad about that, and I've done what I can to make it right. Please forgive me." Or "I made a big mistake that was hard to put right, but I am so grateful for God's forgiveness." Our self-forgiveness makes us more convincing when we say to them, "I can see that you feel sorry for this situation, and you have done your best to correct it and apologize. Now it is time to move on."

Developing true humility. Excessive self-blame keeps us in a one-down position relative to other people. That might not seem so bad if it keeps us humble. But real humility is not about being worse than everyone else. It is about recognizing where we are in relation to God. It also is about acknowledging that we are human like everyone else, subject to weaknesses and failings like all our brothers and sisters. Believing we are worse than others can keep us so focused on our needs, hurts, and failures that instead of getting needed help or helping others, we use our energy to hide or to make others reassure us.

Maintaining hope. Self-forgiveness leads us away from hopelessness and despair that can actually promote sin. When we are convinced of how disgustingly bad we are, hope seems unreachable. We become more likely to give up and give in to temptation, abandon our responsibilities, lash out in anger at others, or lie to cover failings. Appropriate self-forgiveness gives us the hope to keep trying. Instead of distancing ourselves from those we love, we participate in their lives again.

Refocusing on strengths. Self-forgiveness sets us free from our preoccupations with our weaknesses so we can concentrate on contributing our strengths. These are the attributes that will foster the common good and bless other people. The weeds in our personal garden still need attention, but not at the exclusion of the flowers we are trying to cultivate and share. When we take the risks of growth and service, others benefit from the skills and wisdom we can offer.

Avoiding depression and anger. Self-forgiveness steers us away from depression, anxiety, anger, and resentment, all of which canker relationships. A substantial percentage of people living with a depressed person become depressed themselves. Even when we insist that we don't judge others by our excessively high standards, our children and friends can't help but internalize the messages they see us giving ourselves. Most angry people believe they are just defending themselves against being treated disrespectfully or unfairly, and that viewpoint is sustained by the tacit belief that they are inferior to others. Believing we are less than others just stirs up anger that we then use to hurt other people.

Promoting forgiveness. When I can forgive myself I am more forgiving of others, and they benefit from being treated with compassion and respect. Forgiveness of either self or others emerges naturally from a mind-set of mature acceptance of disappointment. When I can find compassion for the wounded, blind, and disappointing aspects of myself, I can be more empathetic with those same qualities in others. I can better offer others forgiveness and better receive the forgiveness they offer me.

Ending false comparisons. Some of us use self-abasement as a ladder to pseudo-self-esteem. We take the one-up position of being more penitent, lowly, and martyred than others to sneakily promote our superiority. The worse we speak of ourselves, the more we can feel better than those who are more self-promoting. We let others keep injuring us because we "deserve" it, but we really do it to make them look mean and to make us look picked on. We don't fairly negotiate on a basis of equality for what we both want and need. We do good things for the wrong reasons and so don't get the real psychological benefit from our service. In contrast, when we are self-forgiving we put ourselves on an equal playing field with others, whom we are willing to forgive as well. We act responsibly and we expect others to do the same, so we are all more likely to get what we really want and need.

SELF-FORGIVENESS BENEFITS US

Of course, self-forgiveness is good for us too. While we may wish we didn't have to know how really stupid and hurtful we can be, real humility gives us something even more lasting and real than being "the fairest of them all." Humility and self-forgiveness give us the peace of knowing we can still be loved and forgiven even when we have sinned, and even when we will undoubtedly sin again. This sweet assurance makes the risks of mortality worth continuing to take.

Another blessing of self-forgiveness and self-acceptance is that we can do small, reasonable acts of service instead of feeling we have to do some great thing to make up for our faults. We don't have to be better, stronger, busier, more important, or more self-sacrificing than others in order to compensate for our enormous failures, all the while believing that we can never really succeed at these bigger-than-life things because we have already proven our badness. When we can receive the forgiveness God offers us, it can be enough to allow us to do ordinary things without trying to be superman or superwoman. We can take satisfaction and pleasure in commonplace goodness.

Finally, as we forgive and accept ourselves we avoid the sin of believing Satan instead of God about our status, worth, and potential. God's forgiveness is a reality that Satan tries to hide from us. The whole rationale for submitting to mortality evaporates if we cannot trust in the power of God to forgive us. Not trusting in His will and power to save us leaves us in a world dominated by Satan's lies, not God's truths.

SELF-BLAME'S SNEAKY BENEFITS

Despite the benefits of self-forgiveness, we do not universally trust that it is really such a good idea. In fact, we often harbor secret doubts about the wisdom of letting ourselves off the hook of self-blame. Self-recrimination has some sneaky advantages we have to see through in order to give them up. Even though we tell ourselves we are afraid self-forgiveness will give us license to sin, we may also punish, berate, and dislike ourselves as a sneaky way to cling to our sin rather than do something about it. Let's look at some examples of the phony advantages of self-flagellation:

- Getting others off our backs—"I'm so sorry I let you down again. I can never forgive myself. I'm so bad at things like this I just shouldn't even try." (Read: "Don't expect much from me because this is all you get.")
- Whipping ourselves before God does—"I'm really a disgusting mess. I'd better shape up fast before God throws the book at me." (Read: "Don't hurt me, God. I'm not worth the trouble. See how despicable I am! Go hurt somebody else.")
- Bolstering self-esteem or feelings of superiority by expecting perfection of ourselves—"How could I be so awful as to cut five minutes off my scripture-reading time just to eat breakfast!" (Read: "What an exceptionally good person I am to worry about such a small matter." Or: "Others are allowed to be more casual about their obedience, but I should always be better than others.")
- Side-stepping the difficult job of real change—"I absolutely must stop gambling like this. My wife will kill me. I'll be bankrupt in a year. I'm going to ruin my life if I keep this up." (Read: "I have no idea why I'm doing this, and I don't really want to go to the trouble or take the risk of making a plan, asking for help, reversing my decision, or digging a little deeper into my psyche, so I'll just try to

scare myself into never doing this again and hope it works for a change.")

Which of these sneaky benefits of self-blame might you be prone to? You might want to check it off on the summary list at the end of this chapter.

MANAGING REGRET, RESPONSIBILITY, AND CONFESSION

Of course, I'm not trying to suggest that there are no legitimate reasons for seriously regretting our mistakes. In fact, regret is an invaluable and necessary step in the repentance process. Christ commends the penitent publican who beats his chest and condemns the self-justifying Pharisee who boasts of his superior righteousness (see Luke 18:9–14). But that does not mean Christ expects or wants us to keep beating our chests endlessly. The breast-beater in the story goes down to his house at the end of the day "justified," that is, "free from blame or guilt" (according to Webster's)[1]—and freedom from blame or guilt does not suggest endless rounds of more breast-beating. In fact, it suggests feeling forgiven, at peace.

We get to the blessings of self-forgiveness through the path of repentance, which includes regretting the harm we've done, taking responsibility for our behavior, confessing our wrongdoing, and apologizing. Unfortunately, regret, responsibility, and confessing can also be taken to unhealthy extremes that interfere with self-forgiveness instead of promoting it. Let's see how.

EXCESSIVE SHAME

One underlying cause of clinging to our self-proclaimed badness is confusing shame and guilt. While we use the words shame and guilt almost interchangeably, psychologists often distinguish between them as a way of separating self-condemnation that leads to improvement from self-condemnation that does not. We will be using this more specialized distinction in this book.

Shame is a natural emotional response to being rejected for violating group norms (which can be as serious as "Don't steal" or as trivial as "Don't put your elbows on the table"). It is akin to embarrassment. We feel shame or embarrassment for being late to a meeting or burping at a formal dinner, but there is nothing inherently wrong with lateness or burping and we wouldn't necessarily feel bad about them if other people weren't watching (unless our shame habit is unusually strong). We can also feel shame for serious sin— worrying more about what others think than about what harm we have done.

The young of many species fear being cast out of the pack they depend upon to survive. Horses and dogs use shaming to capitalize on this fear to socialize younger animals and preserve order. Humans are not so different. As children we learn to internalize shaming messages to keep ourselves in line and avoid punishment. Worrying about our parents' rejection helps keep us in line even when they are not around to enforce the rules. Demonstrating our shame signals to others that we realize we have acted inappropriately and don't need further rejection to teach us a lesson.

When others have shamed us in extreme ways or over a long time, shame can also leave us feeling deeply defective—almost as if we were not even of the same species as the rest of the human family. This self-hatred can run very deep. It becomes the hot, stinging feeling that we associate with being seen, or even imagining being seen, in all our socially unacceptable inadequacies. Instead of making us want to show we are worthy to rejoin the "pack," self-hatred makes us want to distance ourselves from other people or construct masks of exaggerated goodness to hide behind. We fear being seen as the horrible humans we think we really are, unlike the "good" people around us. Extreme shame motivates us to hide.

If shame follows violating group norms or feeling inherently defective as a person, guilt is the more mature, heartfelt regret we feel for specific acts that hurt other people or violate our moral values. Unlike shame, we may feel guilt for yelling at a child or lying to a friend even if we never get caught. Mature guilt includes both holding ourselves accountable for wrongdoing and feeling empathy for those we've harmed. We feel guilt for behavior that hurts innocent people or breaks our personal standards, not for things that merely inconvenience others' social sensibilities. Guilt is what responsible people feel when they both know they have done something wrong and believe that this wrongdoing does not represent who they truly are or what they truly value. Guilt motivates us to repent—to change, confess, reconcile with those we've hurt, and distance ourselves from our wrong behavior instead of from other people.

When we violate our moral code, we can feel either shame or guilt (or neither or both). When we overblame ourselves, taking undue responsibility for a problem or dwelling on our failures instead of learning from them, we produce excessive, counterproductive shame. We feel more concern for how others will think of us than healthy sorrow for the damage we have caused and the violation of our moral code. Instead of helping us take responsibility, change, make amends, and move forward—the very purpose of appropriate and healthy guilt—excessive shame can cause us to bog down in hiding, self-justification, or self-hatred.

Why would we do this to ourselves? Why would we choose unhealthy shame and self-recrimination instead of constructive guilt and repentance? Before you jump to feeling ashamed of feeling ashamed, let me emphasize that shame has a constructive role in human development. Shame is a powerful motivator, and some very good people have gotten that way by having very sensitive shame buttons—albeit at a high personal price. We often don't choose shame so much as fall into shame because it was expected and reinforced in our family or because we have very sensitive temperaments. Parenting efforts that overemphasize shaming instead of calm enforcement of natural consequences can encourage shame and hiding instead of taking responsibility for our behavior. If the price of honesty is too much shaming and rejection, children will naturally cover up their wrongdoings instead of admitting them and making them right.

Another reason we choose shame over guilt is that we don't know there is a real option. Confusing shame and guilt, we think shame is required for real repentance. Perhaps we haven't really seen people take responsibility for their wrongdoing without disintegrating into deep shame. If all our models are shame-based, we assume that admitting wrongdoing is the equivalent of admitting that one is a totally worthless and despicable subhuman. Then when we err, the shame autopilot takes over unless we make a conscious and determined effort to override it.

REINING IN EXCESSIVE SHAME

When we have truly repented and made amends, fresh bouts of shame or anxiety do not necessarily mean we have not been forgiven. Some of us are so sensitized to shame that any trigger event reminding us of our failings chucks us back into the toxic dump of old shame. Rather than assuming we can never achieve forgiveness, we may need to focus on healing old trauma or resisting a predisposition to obsessive-compulsive patterns. (See section 3 of this book.)

Meanwhile, it is useful to remember that excessive shame does not help us stay hopefully and constructively focused on improving. Nor does it help us tune in to the feelings of others. Instead it keeps us preoccupied with the unchangeable past, our own pain, and our fear of other people's judgments.

To get unstuck, we need to affirm our right to like ourselves despite imperfections. We can consciously strengthen our belief in our worth, sidestep excessive preoccupation with embarrassment or shame, and remind ourselves that admitting mistakes is a sign of strength and not weakness. We can urge ourselves instead onto the path of appropriate guilt and repentance: taking responsibility for our behavior, apologizing, changing, making restitution, and acting to regain the trust of those we have wronged. As we do this we can pat ourselves on the back for our courage instead of berating ourselves for being so subhuman as to err.

EXCESSIVE GUILT

So if guilt is more helpful than shame, is it possible to feel too much guilt—to feel too responsible and work too hard to change? I think the answer is yes. While most of us are inclined to take too little responsibility for our contributions to a problem, a few of us will overemphasize our own faults and responsibility as a way to maintain a false sense of control.

For example, let's say we face a problem that others control more than we do, or a problem we cannot imagine how to change short of rewriting our history or changing our biology (which of course we cannot do). Such situations can make us feel out of control, because frankly we are!

As humans we come prewired to look for cause-and-effect patterns so we can use these "rules" to get what we want. But sometimes there simply are no clear rules for changing things that still affect us in painful and powerful ways. In our search for causality—for understanding what causes what so we can get out of pain—we may overfocus on things we can control (like our own failings) rather than on what is really causing the problem (which may have little to do with us). We may see ourselves as more responsible and in control than we really are.

While there is almost always *something* about a problem situation that we can work on, there may also be things we simply do not control. Overemphasizing our faults may make us feel temporarily more in control, but when things don't change we can end up spiraling down into more and more self-recrimination and despair.

For example, a man with marital problems may realize that both he and his wife contribute to the difficulties. He may legitimately and appropriately focus on his own contributions, feel regret, and try to change. But if his wife is entrenched in infidelity or abuse, the marital problems will persist despite all his efforts, leaving him feeling out of control and helpless even though he is working hard to make things better. By focusing undue attention on his own faults and contributions to the problem he may temporarily feel more in control, but in the long run his self-blame may be unrealistic and damaging, leading to false conclusions such as, "If my spouse doesn't respond when I'm working so hard, then I must not be worth much."

Or let's consider people who are victims of physical abuse, who unwittingly cause car accidents, or who get debilitating illnesses—in other words, people with things in their history or biology that they cannot make go away and that have a big impact. Such a person may see these things affect her behavior, identity, relationships, and future choices in ways she doesn't like and doesn't want. She feels life's precariousness, and the world feels chaotic and unsafe. It is scary and disorienting to realize that bad things can happen to her just because she is young and foolish or old and powerless or simply human and subject to illness or chance. She may feel desperate to regain a sense of control, order, and fairness.

Without conscious intent, she may start to take responsibility for what happened to her as a way of regaining control. If she believes her father hit her because she was too loud (instead of because he was out of control), then she can be quieter and maybe not get hit, and the world will feel less unpredictable. If she decides she caused the car accident because she was laughing too much with friends (rather than just inexperienced behind the wheel), then she can stop laughing and stop being with friends and maybe such terrible things won't happen again. If she concludes she got diabetes because God was punishing her for jealousy of her sister, then she can work overtime to make sure never to call attention to herself and make sure her sister gets all the attention. If she can't figure out a specific action or feeling to avoid, then she may simply blame herself for some indiscriminate badness for being angry that these things happened to her. These decisions help her feel more in control in an out-of-control world. These decisions can also have little or nothing to do with who was really responsible for what or with real cause-and-effect relationships. Her attention gets focused in a superstitious way on things that she thinks she can control, not necessarily on what is real. But at least the world does not feel quite so erratic.

REINING IN GUILT

Anxiety often underlies excessive guilt and responsibility. Anxiety serves us well when it helps us anticipate and avoid pain. But anxiety can also make us obsessive, perfectionist, and unrealistic about how much control we really have. It can get us so focused on preventing future problems that we are unable to enjoy the moment. It can get us so focused on staying safely in control that we deny the inherent haphazardness and chaos in the world. Anxiety can get us so terrified of being responsible for anything going wrong that we become paralyzed. Ironically, anxiety escalates in direct proportion to how much we try to control all of the uncontrollable things that make us feel anxious. The more we try to control the uncontrollable the more out of control we feel.

The paradoxical antidote to excessive guilt and anxiety is to increase our tolerance for being wrong, at fault, or out of control. We do this by increasing our trust in God's capacity to make all things, even bad things, work together for good. We can increase our tolerance for being out of control by consciously choosing to accept that even the best people have bad things happen to them, are not universally liked, and do not always succeed. Our anxiety will actually diminish as we stop fighting it by trying to be faultless to a fault and in control of the uncontrollable. Instead of working overtime to be in control, we work to deepen our trust in both God's love and our own timid toughness. True, we may get hurt again, but we acknowledge that we survived once and can survive again.

EXCESSIVE CONFESSION

Confession (like regret and taking responsibility) is a necessary step of repentance. Healthy confession (either by direct apology or confession to an outside party, such as a priesthood leader) signals to others that we know that what we did was wrong or hurtful. Healthy confession can be a bid for needed help in overcoming our problem. By apologizing or confessing we uphold our allegiance to the standards we have violated. Confession allows us to be known by others and still be accepted and cared for, countering shame and the urge to hide, lest others reject us if they know our failings.

But confession can go awry when mishandled or taken to excess. We may confess to random people not affected by our sin, out of fear that they will eventually find out how awful we are, so we might as well get it over with. Alternately, we may use confession to buy brownie points in the game of "see how worldly cool I am" or even "see how far I've come." In any case, excessive or inappropriate confession interferes with the blessings of self-forgiveness.

We can also use confession in a self-defeating way if we substitute confession for real change. If confession is used simply to get us off the hook and help us feel better but is not followed by the other steps of repentance, then it becomes an empty gesture. A young man who calls his bishop at 6:00 A.M. to ruefully confess last night's sexual misconduct may be truly repentant and ready to do whatever it takes to make things right. If he makes a similar call the following month, and again the month after that, then confession may be a way to relieve the stress of guilt or shame without having to go to the trouble of avoiding temptation, gaining insight into himself, admitting his need for help before (not after) sin, or suffering legitimate consequences for his choices.

We can also say "I'm sorry" or "I goofed" without communicating at all that we understand the harm we have done. Our tone of voice or body language can communicate that we are going through the motions of apology without real regret. Such confessions generally cause more problems than they solve because they feel manipulative and insincere. Such confessions can be a cheap substitute for real empathy and sincere apology.

REINING IN CONFESSION

If you are one who overconfesses, consider asking yourself before you confess:

+ If my usual pattern is to confess as soon as possible to relieve my guilty feelings, am I willing instead to wait three days and make an appointment to meet with the person I will confess to? This will help me learn from my errors rather than just unload them and forget them.
+ Is the person I am considering confessing to someone who is harmed by my behavior or responsible for helping me? If not, I probably need to keep quiet now and confess to the appropriate person.
+ Am I confessing as a way of either feeling special or relieving my anxiety? If so, what is a more appropriate way to boost self-esteem or soothe anxious feelings?
+ What have I learned from this slip that I didn't know or do before? If I haven't learned something new or really attempted to put what I've learned into action, then learning and action, not more confession, are what I should work on.
+ How can I use my confession to gain support and strengthen my accountability for my actions? Greater accountability and change are the goals.

HEALTHY SHAME, GUILT, AND CONFESSION

Shame, guilt, and confession—though painful and dysfunctional when out of hand—can serve important functions that we do not want to lose. Normal shame can motivate us to be sensitive to others' expectations and not become a law unto ourselves. Healthy guilt must be endured if we are to both uphold our own ideals and keep trying when we fall short. Confession helps us take responsibility for hurting someone and then work to make things right.

Healthy people endure a certain amount of shame in order to contain their antisocial impulses and remain in the group. Healthy people endure a certain amount of anxiety in order to take needed risks and grow. Healthy people endure appropriate guilt in order to acknowledge mistakes and improve, take responsibility for making things right, and empathize with the pain they cause others. Healthy people confess their wrongdoings, accept responsibility for them, and sincerely apologize when they have hurt another. Ideally, we learn to take these steps without sliding into self-hatred, cynicism, hopelessness, and obsession. We come to accept imperfection, lack of control, and the unchangeable nature of the past without loss of basic trust in ourselves and life.

In the summary at the end of the chapter, rate yourself on shame, guilt, and confessing.

DEEP ASSUMPTIONS UNDERPINNING SELF-FORGIVENESS

Getting to self-forgiveness may require giving up our overidealized self-image, our freedom to do exactly as we please, and our naïve insistence on life as we once knew it. Lasting self-forgiveness requires more than changed behavior. It also requires changing our mind and heart and acquiring a fresh view of how life works. Self-forgiveness means:

+ *Accepting that few people get through life without betraying, deceiving, or harming someone they love, and that we are not among those few people.* This is more than a philosophical abstract, but a personal "aha!" about the nature of life and the nature of our own lives. Good intentions are not enough to keep us from hurting people we deeply care about. This is the nature of life.

+ *Relinquishing the erroneous belief that we are good enough to avoid any serious weakness or sin.* The painful truth is that we are subject to sin and weakness like everyone else, and our sins and weaknesses have real consequences. Humility requires accepting that we have less power, control, wisdom, or goodness than we had hoped and that these are not what earn us safety or love.

+ *Giving up all hope of ever having a better past.* While this seems obvious, much of our angst about our sin is really angry insistence that we can be happy again only if God turns back the clock on our failures. God's supernal power to bring good out of bad does not include making things as they were before our error. When we give up all hope of having a better past, we can begin working toward a new normal instead of fighting pointlessly for a return to the old normal.

+ *Knowing and curbing rather than denying or indulging our capacity for harm.* Self-forgiveness means getting to know our dark side and doing something about it—not convincing ourselves we don't have one or that it is too powerful to rein in. We sort out why we did what we did, make and keep promises to ourselves and others, and stay away from trouble rather than assuming we can handle it.

+ *Choosing to focus on the positive in ourselves.* Although we recognize our weaknesses, we turn our attention to contributing from our strengths. We organize our time and energy to develop our gifts, not take false comfort in obsessing about our flaws.

+ *Choosing to trust the resilience of others.* We expect ourselves to take responsibility for our choices even when we are hurt by life, and we humbly allow others the same opportunity when they have been hurt by us. We do all we can to make things right and then accept that others have choices to make as well.

+ *Being vigilant about our choices so others won't have to be.* We protect those we've harmed from worry rather than expecting them to act like nothing happened. We work to earn trust rather than seeing it as our right. We are honest about our temptations and what we are doing to avoid and resist them. We are solicitous of the comfort of others without going so far overboard that we make it about us again.

+ *Giving up mental conversations and images focused on our mistakes.* When we find our minds looping endlessly through old scenarios, we ask ourselves, "Am I learning anything new here?" If not, we gently but firmly turn our attention to other things.

+ *Stopping thoughts of self-punishment and worries about shameful exposure or others' revenge.* We stop scaring ourselves with what others might think or do to us, and we stop yelling at ourselves inside of our heads. We stop sabotaging ourselves, hurting ourselves, threatening ourselves, or neglecting ourselves. We treat ourselves with respect.

+ *Accepting God's assurance that our debt has been canceled.* We choose to take God's word that we have done what we can to put things right, and we mentally write across our debt, "Paid." We never forget that Christ is the one who has paid our debt, and we also give ourselves credit for having done what we can. Our lives reflect our deep gratitude and submission to God.

+ *Investing our energy in hopeful possibilities for the future.* We choose to turn our attention away from the past and toward building better societies to support the values we have come to deeply appreciate. We help others not make the same mistakes or be vulnerable to the same temptations. We build trusting relationships and let ourselves believe that other people like and accept us.[2]

Which of these steps are you doing pretty well at? At the end of the chapter, check the ones you are making good progress on believing most of the time. Circle the ones you really need to work on at this time.

RECEIVING THE GIFT

When Christ appeared to the Nephites after His resurrection, He summarized His entire message of salvation in just five words. He explained, "And this is my doctrine, and it is the doctrine which the Father hath given unto me; . . . and I bear record that the Father commandeth all men, everywhere, to *repent and believe in me*" (3 Nephi 11:32; emphasis added). This is His most fundamental commandment to each of us: repent and believe in Him. What does it mean to believe in Christ? Surely it is not just to believe that there was a man named Jesus who was the Son of God. To believe in Christ is to trust in His atonement as sufficient for "all men, everywhere," including us.

Receiving God's forgiveness and extending forgiveness to ourselves is therefore a commandment and a righteous goal, not just self-indulgence. As with all our righteous goals, we will not be perfect at this one. Nevertheless, it is a goal worth striving for and working toward, recognizing that when we fail to accept the proffered gift of grace we do not sufficiently honor God. The more trustingly and humbly we receive this gift, the more it pleases the Lord. Mercy is at the very essence of who God is. It is a worthy effort on our part to stretch our capacity to know Him in all His goodness, to trust Him more fully, to emulate His generosity and kindness more completely, and to accept His gifts more gratefully and joyfully. If we have repented but do not yet believe and receive the Atonement, then we still have a ways to go in following Christ completely. We make this effort to receive and trust His forgiveness as a demonstration of our gratitude and trust in Christ, not as a demonstration of trust in ourselves.

I can imagine someone who struggles to really receive God's mercy thinking, "Swell, I'm so imperfect that I'm even imperfect at being imperfect. Now I just feel guilty that I continue to feel guilty!" Yes—we *are* imperfect *even at accepting being imperfect.* So this is as good a thing as any to practice not berating ourselves for. Instead we should humbly accept our imperfection as a weakness of the mortal condition that we may struggle with. And even in this God can show us mercy and love. Even this we are given room to grow into. Even in our failure to receive His mercy for our failures, He will gently lead us along, blessing us and those we love.

SUMMARY EXERCISE

How is your balance sheet stacking up of reasons for or against self-forgiveness? Which of the reasons to forgive yourself feel most important to remember? People are more apt to sustain change when the advantages for making the change outweigh the disadvantages.

BLESSINGS TO OTHERS OF SELF-FORGIVENESS

Which of the following advantages to others of your self-forgiveness are most meaningful to you?

- ☐ Modeling self-forgiveness for those I love.
- ☐ Being humble—neither one up nor one down with others so I'm not making my needs their priority.
- ☐ Maintaining hope so I won't be as likely to give up and give in to temptation.
- ☐ Focusing on my strengths so I can develop and contribute them to others.
- ☐ Avoiding depression and anger, which make me hard to live with.
- ☐ Promoting forgiveness and being better able to forgive others.
- ☐ Ending false comparisons by making myself look bad to make others look worse.

BLESSINGS TO OURSELVES OF SELF-FORGIVENESS

Which of the following advantages of self-forgiveness are most worth seeking for you?

- ☐ Increasing genuine self-esteem based on accurate self-assessment rather than superiority over others.
- ☐ Making righteousness feel more doable, since ordinary acts of service and goodness become enough.
- ☐ Increasing my trust in God's truths about His willingness to forgive instead of believing Satan's lies that only perfection will suffice.

PSEUDO-ADVANTAGES OF SELF-BLAME

Which of the pseudo-advantages of self-blame are you most tempted to fall for?

☐ Getting people off my back.
☐ Whipping myself before God does.
☐ Bolstering my self-esteem by expecting perfection.
☐ Sidestepping the difficulty of real change.

MANAGING SHAME, GUILT, AND CONFESSION

Where would you rate yourself on the following scales:

Excessive shame   **Healthy shame**   Not enough shame

Overworry about how   Don't care how I'm seen
others see me   by others

Excessive guilt   **Healthy guilt**   Not enough guilt

Take too much responsi-   Avoid responsibility and
bility and blame myself   blame others

Overconfess or   **Confess/apologize**   Rarely confess
apologize   **appropriately**   or apologize

Deep Assumptions That Underpin Self-Forgiveness

Which of these deep assumptions do you fully believe and integrate into your life? Which ones do you most need to work on now?

- ☐ Accepting that few people get through life without betraying, deceiving, or harming someone they love, and that I am *not* one of those few people.
- ☐ Relinquishing the erroneous belief that I am powerful enough to be free from ignorance, weakness, or sin.
- ☐ Giving up all hope of ever having a better past.
- ☐ Knowing and curbing rather than denying or indulging my capacity for harm.
- ☐ Choosing to focus on the positive in myself and the resilience of others.
- ☐ Being vigilant about my choices so others won't have to be.
- ☐ Giving up mental conversations and images focused on my mistakes.
- ☐ Stopping thoughts of self-punishment and worries about shameful exposure or others' revenge.
- ☐ Accepting God's assurance that my debt has been canceled.
- ☐ Investing my energy in hopeful possibilities for the future.

PART 2

QUALIFYING FOR FORGIVENESS

Faith in Christ's atoning power to save and succor us develops as we understand the plan of salvation. We can afford to hope that God's grace can apply even to us as we understand His purpose for our mortality. We can also afford to contemplate forgiving ourselves, not only to benefit ourselves but others as well. We now turn our attention to the process of repentance that qualifies us for God's forgiveness and our own forgiveness. Chapter 4 in this section helps us with the crucial distinction between what we need to repent of and what we need to accept more. Chapter 5 will explore questions about the challenges of repentance and growth.

4

WHO DONE IT?

*Forgiving and being reconciled are not about
pretending that things are other than they are. It is not
patting one another on the back and turning a blind eye
to the wrong. . . . Forgiveness . . . means taking what
happened seriously and not minimizing it; drawing out
the sting in the memory that threatens to poison our
entire existence. It involves trying to understand the
perpetrators and so have empathy, to try to stand in their
shoes and appreciate the sort of pressures and influences
that might have conditioned them.*

—DESMOND TUTU[1]

THE PROBLEMS

The things we struggle to forgive ourselves for range from the
trifling to the tragic, from silly misunderstandings to serious malfea-
sance. I have struggled to forgive myself for everything from violating a fundamental trust to dropping a piece of chicken (it's a long
story). Other examples:

+ A graduate student who cannot forgive himself for failing his qualifying exams
+ A parent who agonizes over past parenting foibles when a child turns to drugs and crime
+ A convert whose baptism does not relieve her shame and sorrow about an abortion decades before
+ A man who tears up about not making it to his dying grandfather's bedside thirty years ago
+ A teacher who berates herself for years for forgetting a lonely child's birthday
+ A brother who feels ashamed to return to Church activity when others might be aware of his past
+ A rape victim who condemns herself for being in the wrong place at the wrong time
+ A husband who grovels in self-recrimination for not making more money
+ A missionary who blames his failure to get up on time two days in a row on his investigator for deciding not to get baptized
+ A young mother filled with regret for neglecting her genealogy
+ A husband who blames himself for cheating on his taxes and excuses himself for cheating on his wife
+ A visiting teacher who berates herself for not magnifying her calling

Some of these people have sinned and need heartfelt repentance before self-forgiveness can follow. Some have made poor judgment calls and simply need to learn from their mistakes, apologize, and move on. Still others demonstrate a human weakness, suggesting the need for patient self-improvement more than penitent self-reform.

And some have done absolutely nothing wrong, though they may continue to feel responsible or sullied. They need to determine if they need repentance and self-forgiveness, humility and self-acceptance, or healing and forgiveness of others.

So let's consider The Case of the Dropped Chicken, an incident for which I had trouble forgiving myself for years. We are overdue for a little comic relief, so this is the story (which was not at all funny at the time!).

I was on a plane with my son, Mike, who was about three, back in the days when airlines actually served hot food. The flight attendant handed me the last hot chicken dinner from her cart and then went back for others. I started cutting up the chicken, which was in some kind of sugary sauce, feeding myself and my son each a bite as I did so, and planning to pass the meal to him once it was all cut up.

While I was still busy cutting, the flight attendant returned and plopped a freshly cooked dinner in front of my three-year-old, who promptly stuck his fork in the whole chicken breast and dropped it on his bare, shorts-clad leg. When he started to scream I immediately realized that his chicken must be a lot hotter than mine and was burning his leg. I grabbed the meat, but it was in fact so hot that my fingers would not hold it and I dropped it again, right on the same spot, making him scream again. It still makes me shudder to think about it. I grabbed for my napkin and removed the offending chicken, but it had already done its damage. A large blister began to form almost immediately, eventually leaving a half-dollar-sized scar that lasted for many years.

For two decades I could not think about this incident or see that scar without feeling horrible about myself. I'd heard the stories about mothers lifting cars with their bare hands to rescue their trapped children, suffering deprivation of every kind to spare their offspring, fighting off bears and alligators to protect their young—you know the ones. I was a mother who couldn't even hold on to a piece of hot chicken. What kind of a mother is that? A big fat *chicken* mother! I felt terrible about this failure. I couldn't forgive myself.

I still feel really sad that my son got burned so badly. In fact, it can still make me cry to think of his little bare leg blistering under that simmering sauce. I still regret that I could not be the Supermom I wanted to be. But I no longer feel ashamed of what others must think of me or guilty for supposed bad parenting. After going through the self-analysis I am about to take you through, I began to see that I was not responsible for what happened to my son, even though my fingers were the ones to betray him. I can afford to let this one go. I don't need to feel guilty, repent, or forgive myself because in fact I did the best I could with the human, mortal body I live in. I may need to repent of pride—thinking that somehow I should be above the natural instincts of my flesh for self-preservation—but not of being a lousy mother. I have to make peace with being fallible, but not with being bad. Self-acceptance, not self-forgiveness, is called for.

The principles of self-acceptance and self-forgiveness applicable to this less-than-earth-shattering situation can also be applied in more serious situations. I can feel deep regret about another's suffering without feeling shame or responsibility, even when I have inadvertently contributed to that suffering. Genuine repentance always includes regret, but because we feel regret does not always mean we need to repent. That is an important distinction. We can feel really sad about something, even something we had a hand in, without having done anything morally wrong.

Of course, there are other circumstances in which I have been plenty guilty, have had plenty to repent of, and have done plenty wrong that was fully in my control to change. That conclusion calls for a different course of action. But I cannot really decide whether I need deeper acceptance of my human frailties or deeper repentance and contrition until I sort out exactly who is responsible for what. This chapter is about that sorting process. Because, just as in a great whodunit mystery novel, the real culprit is not always easy to distinguish from the red herrings until we see all the clues—even when we think the culprit is us.

If we decide we are the culprit and deserve punishment or need repentance, then chapter 5 will help us get on with the next steps toward constructive change, restitution, or whatever is called for to allow us to repent and move forward. But before we can figure out what to do to repent (the most important part of our personal story, but the part mystery novels never talk about), we need to know who is responsible for what.

MISS SCARLET IN THE CONSERVATORY WITH A REVOLVER

The classic game of *Clue* requires players to use good reasoning skills to determine who committed a murder in what room of a house and with what weapon. We need more than good reasoning to determine our own guilt or innocence, however—we need the Lord's Spirit. God alone can discern the thoughts and intents of our hearts, the motives, circumstances, personal histories, and genetic makeup that affect our actions—and our guilt or innocence. But we can prayerfully consider a few questions to help us determine if we need more repentance, more self-acceptance, or both. Those questions include:

+ What went wrong?
+ Who was harmed and how?

+ Who is responsible?
+ What, if anything, do I need to change?

Let's apply these questions to The Case of the Dropped Chicken. For years I answered all four questions by saying I dropped hot chicken on my son's leg, he got burned, it was my fault, and if he is ever so imperiled again I need to keep that chicken from burning him, even at the peril of my life. Seems clear enough. So clear in fact, that for almost two decades I had convicted myself of child abuse, parental ineptitude, and moral failure for my crime. But a more careful analysis led me to a different conclusion. Let's take these questions one at a time.

WHAT WENT WRONG?

First, we need to be specific about what went wrong in order to determine what needs to change. I was pretty clear about what went wrong in this situation, but in some situations it is a lot fuzzier. Staying fuzzy about what we did wrong blocks real change. For example, let's say Tom can't forgive himself for being a bad parent because his child has a drug problem. Telling himself he was a bad parent is not enough because it doesn't tell Tom how or what to change. He is simply stuck in the unchangeable past with his unalterable regrets, feeling irreversibly bad about himself.

But once he is clear about what went wrong he has a start on how to change, to repent: "I didn't have regular family home evenings, I didn't manage my own depression, and I didn't help my kids make friends." Okay—now Tom is beginning to get something he can work with. This doesn't mean he will instantly feel better once he specifies these things—in fact, he may feel worse! But at least he is on the road toward repentance and self-forgiveness. Even though his kids are grown, he can still look for ways to make his own life accord more closely with his truest values. As he does so he can qualify for the blessings of repentance, show his kids a better example, and stop feeling so hopeless and helpless about a past he cannot undo.[2]

Back at The Case of the Dropped Chicken, I need to answer the question, "What went wrong?" I need to consider the question honestly and objectively, like a good detective reenacting the crime. Who was where? Who did what? What happened when? If the situation I'm analyzing is long or complex, like a failed marriage or a history of dishonesty at work, then I need to specify what I did that I should not have done, what I didn't do that I should have done, what justifications I used for my behavior, and what others did to contribute. As I lay out the story matter-of-factly, I start to see who was responsible for what.

WHO WAS HARMED AND HOW?

The second question, "Who was harmed and how?" is pretty cut and dried in The Case of the Dropped Chicken but less clear with vaguer crimes like "I'm not patient enough" or "I'm a lousy neighbor." I need to know the nature of the "debt" I incurred and with whom before I can begin to make plans to pay it back, declare bankruptcy and negotiate a settlement, or turn the debt to Christ. I need to know what I took that did not belong to me and to distinguish what I took from what others took. I cannot repent for other people's failures, or repent for something I don't need to accept responsibility for. A clear sense of who was harmed and how helps me know how to make restitution for my sin.

Sometimes another's injury is not as clear-cut as a blistered leg. If I am not certain someone was really harmed by my behavior, I can ask them or others close to them for more information. I can make it easier for someone to be honest with me if I say, "If I had been in your shoes I might have felt . . . Is that what you felt?" Sometimes we feel terrible about something that did not bother the other person at all; other times we barely notice a problem while the other person is upended. We can't clear these things up unless we know who is hurt and how.

Knowing how others are hurt also reinforces why we should bother changing. Looking carefully at who was hurt and how helps us develop real empathy with those we injured. True empathy changes our hearts, not just our behavior. We are much more likely to eschew evil and claim good when we truly understand how others were hurt as a result of our actions. Without this empathy we can act with impunity in sinful or thoughtless ways, not letting ourselves know and feel the emotional damage we are doing. You'll see more on this below under "When Will We Ever Learn?"

Even if we did not commit a terrible sin in our own estimation, our empathy for someone we offended or hurt helps them feel heard and cared about so they will have an easier time healing. I remember a Church leader who listened patiently to my irritation with his handling of an administrative issue. I was very hurt and put off by what happened but also nervous about trying to clear the air. He was completely empathetic with my frustration and apologetic for the problem, even though when all the facts were in he had not done what I thought he had. His patience, listening, and empathy—even when he had not done anything wrong—went a long way to soothe my hurt feelings and restore my respect.

WHO IS RESPONSIBLE?

The third question, "Who is responsible?" is a complicated one but is at the crux of this little analysis. To answer it, I may first need to consider multiple options. In The Case of the Dropped Chicken,

the airline, the flight attendant, my son, and I are the potential culprits. My son is the immediate agent of the harm caused—after
all, he dropped the chicken. But even a bunch of kids playing *Clue*
would probably not hold a three-year-old responsible for this
"crime." The flight attendant put the hot chicken in front of a child,
so perhaps she is responsible for not checking its temperature. Or
perhaps the airline is responsible for not training her better about
poultry hazards in flight. We can get closer to identifying who is
morally responsible, not just *causally* responsible, as we consider
people's intentions, capacity for judgment, amount of control, and
ability to foresee the outcomes of their behavior. We may also need
to consider the nature of the contract broken by a person's act. When
I break the law, break the commandments, break my word, break an
implicit contract with someone I love, or break the social codes I
otherwise support, my responsibility for wrongdoing increases.

WHAT DO I NEED TO CHANGE?

This responsibility question also helps us determine what we are
personally responsible for, leading to the fourth question, "What do
I need to change?" This was the dead-giveaway question for me
because I realized there wasn't anything I would expect myself to
change should a similar situation arise in the future. Based on my
experience with the first piece of chicken in the airplane, I had no
reason to think my son's chicken would be dangerous to his health
and well-being. I had no intention of hurting him. I had minimal
control over either the flight attendant's actions or my son's. I had
previously assumed that a really good mother would not selfishly
drop burning chicken back onto her son's leg. But unless I were to
take up hot-coal-walking to develop my capacity for deep trance
states of mind over body on a moment's notice, I probably would not

be able to perform any differently the next time my toddler got handed a sizzling chicken breast while helplessly constrained in an airplane seat—which in fact never happened again and is not likely to now that airlines serve nothing hotter than chipotle pretzels.

Considering how I need to change leads me to conclude either (1) "I did the best I could under the circumstances," or (2) "In the future I will change . . ." I can begin to accept that there are some things I simply cannot control, or I can begin to take control of things I can change. As I look at what I need to change, I can further explore whether my current failure is the result of pride, rebellion, or disobedience to God (requiring repentance) or human limitation and weakness (requiring humility and learning). In either case, once I answer this question I can begin to let go of the past and move forward with a plan for the future. I can focus on what I've learned, not just how I failed. In this case, I learned to be more vigilant about potentially hot food in the hands of toddlers. I also learned that burns heal, tears dry, and children forgive, thank goodness. And I learned real empathy for others I might meet who have caused harm to someone else and feel devastated for it even though it was not really their fault. All of these lessons have value to me.

LET'S GET STARTED

So now that I've explained the rules, let's see if they can help you identify the responsible parties at your own crime scene. I assume you've already figured out some things you carry around that eat at your conscience or your self-image—otherwise you probably wouldn't be reading this book. So think of some things that can make you feel bad about yourself. List them in the first column below. They might include really big failings or small incidents that others have long since forgotten. If you have more than four, write the rest in the margins to come back to later. If you have more than twenty, then stick to those that happened in the past week or past month. This process will work better if you write things down, so if you don't want to scribble on your book, just get out a sheet of paper or open a blank page on your computer.

1. What are some things you have trouble forgiving yourself for? In the left column, write down a key phrase for each.

A. Issue	B. Distress	C. Nature

2. In the B column, rate how much distress you feel about that issue (1=low to 10=high).

3. In the C column, indicate if you personally broke a law, commandment, personal value, implicit contract with another person, or social code for this situation (you might have broken more than one), or put a 0 if you didn't really break any of these.

L = broke a law   S = broke a social code
C = broke a commandment   0 = none of the above
V = violated a personal value
IC = broke an implicit contract

Choose one of these problem issues from column A to focus on right now and put a check by it. Use this issue for the rest of the questions.

4. Who was the primary person who was hurt in this situation (it might be you)? What did this person lose because of what happened? (Consider things such as health, feeling of safety, dreams, self-image, trust, belongings, money, time, relationships, options, work, hope, faith, self-confidence, opportunities, healing, needed help, innocence, reputation, emotional well-being, love, protection, honest answers, feeling included, opportunity to grieve, feeling important.)

Person hurt: _____

What the person lost:

_____

_____

_____

_____

_____

This is an important list. This list of debts owed has to be dealt with for justice to be done. At minimum, others deserve honest acknowledgment and genuine empathy for their losses before we can rightly forgive ourselves if we are responsible for the damage.

In The Case of the Dropped Chicken, my son was the one harmed. He lost a pain-free leg, some healthy skin tissue, and some of his sense of safety and trust in adults. If I decide I am the responsible party, then this is the debt I owe. I won't be able to do much about his skin tissue, but I can doctor his leg, offer empathy and explanations, and work to restore his trust. These efforts help to pay back what he lost.

We often lose something as well in these interactions. For

example, I lost my self-image as a mother who would sacrifice any-thing to protect her child. In other situations the one I hurt may have hurt me too. We are both in debt to each other. I might blame myself for impatience, but say the coworker I lose patience with is repeatedly late with important work. My impatience costs my coworker, but he costs me something as well. So let's put down our own losses too, both self-imposed and imposed by others.

What I lost:

_____

_____

_____

What others took from me:

_____

_____

_____

In The Case of the Dropped Chicken, the part of me that lost her self-image as Supermom is the part of me that wouldn't forgive me for what happened. That Supermom wannabe held the fallible, human part of me hostage for messing up her dreams of motherhood infallibility. That unforgiving part of me is like a kid who has not quite grown up to face the real limitations of being a real adult in a real world. She still thinks she should never have to face the indignity of doing anything wrong. Sometimes the Superperson wannabe in each of us needs a gentle reminder that any job worth doing (like par-enting or missionary work, charity or faith, growing up or growing old) is too complicated and difficult to do perfectly. I can't on a sec-ond's notice make my body do something it is programmed to instinctively avoid. I won't always have the wisdom, perspective, energy, or experience to handle every situation ideally. If I had had more time to think, maybe I could have made myself pick up that chicken even though it was hot, but it took less time to grab the napkin instead. I made a reasonable choice in the time I had. I can live with being fallible and human, even though I still feel really sad that Mike got hurt.

In other situations, what we lost was more than an exaggerated self-image or an unrealistic dream—things we probably need to lose anyway. When the person we harmed has also harmed us, acknowledging this accurately can help us get past blaming and on to problem solving. Quite simply, validating losses helps people heal. (We still need to be responsible about our own failings, but chapter 5 will also help us negotiate with others for what they took from us.)

5. Who are the people who might share responsibility for the harm caused? Write their names in the left column below. Include yourself and if appropriate the person harmed.

A. Name	B. Action	C. Nature	D. Intent	E. Control

6. Under "Action" write down the most blame-worthy thing each person did. (For example, "Mike—dropped burning chicken on his leg," "Me—didn't hold on to burning chicken," "Flight attendant—didn't assess for excessive chicken temperature before serving," "Airline—didn't train flight attendants in proper chicken management.")

This is your List of Suspects, along with the actions they took or failed to take that might make them *causally* responsible for what happened. Next we need to consider who was *morally* responsible, not just who was in the conservatory holding the revolver when we walked in. The next three columns will help us decipher issues of moral responsibility.

7. In the "Nature" column, indicate the nature of each person's behavior. Was it

(1) a normal human frailty common to our mortal experience?

(2) a judgment call that might or might not have led to a problem, depending on unforeseeable circumstances?

(3) a bad judgment call that was part of a pattern of risky behavior or poor choices the person had been warned about before?

(4) a violation of a commandment, law, or moral contract between two people?

In this situation, I would have to say that my son gets a 1, and I get a 1. The flight attendant and airline get a 2, a 3 if they had already faced multiple cases of chicken burns on previous flights, or a 4 if they had already been found guilty of previous chicken mishandling and had been court-ordered to provide meat thermometers on future flights but had failed to do so.

8. In the "Intent" column, indicate if the person

(1) could not have foreseen the harm their action would cause (or no obvious harm was caused),

(2) might have foreseen the harm caused but hadn't really faced this situation before (or the harm caused was very unlikely in that circumstance),

(3) should have foreseen the harm caused but ignored warnings or experience,

(4) intended the harm caused.

Again, my son and I probably get a 1 and the flight attendants
and airline probably get a 2. It is easier to see our own intentions
than someone else's, so I give others the benefit of any doubt in my
ratings.

9. In the last column, rank the people according to who had the
most direct, personal control over the decisions that led to
harm or damage, with

(1) being the person with the least control
(2) being the person with the next least control
(3) being the person with more control
(4) being the person with the most control

This one is tricky and depends somewhat on how I define control, but I'll give my son the 1, the flight attendant 2, me the 3, and
the airline the 4. Someone else might call it differently, but since I
was the one sitting there and in charge of my son, I feel like I had
more direct control than the flight attendant. But I would probably
say the airline had the most control over what food was served and
how the attendants were told to prepare it.

10. As you look over the above and consider your own situation, decide who you think is most responsible for what
happened that caused harm, and why. Summarize below
whom you hold responsible, and why.

I hold _____ primarily responsible for
_____ because _____

_____

11. How responsible are you, and why? Write below what, if anything, you are personally responsible for doing or failing to do for which repentance is needed.

I hold myself responsible for _____

because _____

_____

I guess if I were going to hold someone responsible it would be the airline, and in fact I turned in a report of the chicken incident to help them realize the risk of future burns and take preventive measures in the future. But I am willing to assume that the harm caused was a normal risk of eating airline food, not unforgivably poor judgment or intentional injury. I can let this go. I also eventually decided that I don't hold myself responsible because I had no reason to think the chicken being handed to my son was excessively hot, I did the best I could to help him despite my normal human frailties, and I was empathetic, compassionate, and responsible in how I handled the accident once it occurred.

The self-forgiveness game is serious business and is not over, but at least now you have identified more clearly who you think is responsible for what in this one situation that has troubled you. Both God and other people can help you clarify your thinking, overcome your blind spots, and see patterns you might otherwise ignore. I highly recommend running your answers past someone else, especially if you are feeling stirred up or unsettled by what you've decided, but also just to test your assessments and keep yourself honest and objective. Especially if you have been told in the past that you are either too hard on yourself or too quick to blame others, ask someone whom you trust to be both kind and impartial to review your conclusions.

If you are morally responsible for causing harm because you broke a commandment or moral agreement, or because you made a mistake that previous experience or warnings should have told you would result in harm, then repentance is the next step toward self-forgiveness. Chapter 5 will help you take better advantage of this amazing debt-recovery system. If you still feel self-blame for harm you aren't responsible for, or for a nonmoral failure or weakness, then an examination of your beliefs about God (introduction), the meaning of sin or weakness (chapter 2), or an analysis of your self-talk (part 3) may help. But before we leave Miss Scarlet and the Conservatory, let's look at one more smoking gun she might be holding.

WHEN WILL WE EVER LEARN?

Let's say Miss Scarlet is found in the Conservatory with a gun in her hand and a wounded body at her feet. She tearfully claims that the gun went off by accident and wasn't even supposed to be loaded. You are inclined to believe her, but then you learn that Miss Scarlet has been involved with several other "accidental" shootings. She no longer looks so innocent.

We are not so apt to buy our own innocence either if we can't help noticing that we've been in this situation before. We should have learned our lesson, but here we are again, smoking gun in hand, trying to convince someone else that we didn't know the gun was loaded and wondering with shock and horror how we could have let this happen again.

If any of this sounds analogous to one of the situations we can't forgive ourselves for, then another set of questions can help us learn from the past so we don't have to keep hearing our own lame excuses. These questions can be especially helpful when we are dealing with a repeated failure that has taken us by surprise because we didn't see it coming . . . again. It is one thing to forgive someone else or ourselves for an isolated incident; it is quite another when there is a repeated pattern of problematic behavior. To illustrate these additional issues, let's look at a smoking gun Ellie never seems to notice is loaded until it has gone off yet again, hurting someone she loves.

Ellie recently agreed to pick her husband up from the airport. This is a major event for them because she has been late so many times picking him up from the airport that he now insists on taking a taxi instead—a good solution. But because of other plans they had for the evening, he cautiously agreed that she would pick him up. She decided what time she needed to leave home to be at the airport on time (a good start). She didn't build in any extra time for traffic delays, even though she was traveling during a high-traffic time (oops—there's that gun). She "forgot" until the last minute that she had several things she needed to take with her that would take a few minutes to gather up (getting out the ammo). She worked on something she'd agreed to do for a friend until the exact time she needed to leave and then took several more minutes to get ready and get going (loading the gun). She forgot her cell phone in her rush, leaving no way for her to contact her husband or him to contact her (taking off the safety). She did hit the traffic that she had neglected to plan for (taking aim). She got to the airport ten minutes later than she had promised to be there, her husband's plane had gotten in fifteen minutes earlier than expected, and he ended up waiting for twenty-five minutes with no way to reach her (bang!).

If this were the first time she had gotten caught with this smoking gun in her hand, Ellie could justifiably claim it was an accident and expect patience from her husband. But as someone has pointed out, too often "accident" really means "foreseeable outcome of bad judgment." This is not an event but part of a pattern of lateness. So why doesn't she ever learn? Why does she always end up at the airport late, making excuses, ashamed but also irritated with others for being irritated with her for being late? It seems that she doesn't know whether they are to blame for impatience or she is to blame for uncharitable indifference to others' feelings.

Let's look at four questions that can be useful in figuring out why we keep ending up in that same old Conservatory holding yet one more smoking gun.

First question: When have I been the victim in a similar situation, and how was I expected to handle it?

Or if I'm Ellie: "When have I been made to wait, and what was I supposed to do about it?" This is an important question because it helps us see how we have been taught to handle similar problems in the past. Notice that I'm not asking when Ellie has been late before but when others have been late with her. Have others done to her what she is now doing, and how did they expect her to handle it?

Several situations came to mind for Ellie. First, she had indeed waited for others who were late picking her up at airports, and they expected her to be patient and not complain. She had also had to wait for people arriving at airports, circling her car endlessly without being able to tell if their flight was even in. She had waited a lot for her mother, who infuriated Ellie's father with her lateness, and Ellie's mom had expected her to agree that he was being mean and unreasonable. And finally, one of the more hurtful experiences of Ellie's childhood was waiting for many hours for rescue from an accident scene while the adults around her seemed oblivious to her anguish. They had not even realized how confused and upset she was while waiting, so they had acted as if they expected her to pretend she was not waiting at all or that waiting was not a problem.

Second question: What should I have learned from these situations?

Or in Ellie's case: "What should I have learned about what it would be like for my husband if I were late to pick him up?" She *should* have learned that it is really frustrating, anxiety-provoking, and boring to have to wait for someone—especially when you can't reach them to find out what is going on, they have left you in a similar lurch before, you have an event you are scheduled to attend, and they don't really get how frustrated you are. But instead, Ellie pretended that she did not feel any of those things when she had to wait, and that it is mean and unreasonable for others to feel them.

To be fair, part of the problem is that Ellie *has* learned how much she hates waiting, and now she would much rather keep others waiting than wait herself, although she doesn't like to admit to something that feels so selfish. But another part of the problem is that Ellie doesn't really know whether waiting is: (1) an inevitability to be handled with patience or (2) a problem to be tackled, solved, and eliminated. She has often been taught that nice people are just supposed to be patient with waiting, that waiting is inevitable and can't be avoided, and that her dislike of waiting is mean, unreasonable, and selfish—so her dislike of waiting cannot be admitted openly. Her best self-defense against having to wait is to keep others waiting instead, making them the mean and unreasonable ones instead of her. The situation at the airport repeats all these old dynamics but never tackles the problem of how waiting might be avoided or handled constructively.

A more mature solution might include:

+ realizing that since waiting is especially hard for Ellie's husband because she has let him down before, she should make extra effort to plan ahead, communicate, and get there early;

+ realizing that since waiting is especially hard for her, she should take a book, a bag of popcorn, and a cell phone so if she has to wait she won't be bored (and if he has to wait she can let him know she is coming);
+ checking the flight update in advance of leaving to minimize either party having to wait at all.

More to the point, what Ellie has *not* learned is real empathy for either herself or others. She doesn't really think about how much she hates waiting or how much others probably hate waiting—she just ignores the whole situation while she sets herself up to repeat it.

Third question: What kept me from learning that lesson?

For Ellie: "What kept me from having enough empathy for my husband to do everything possible not to make him wait?" For Ellie there are multiple barriers to learning, as is the case with most stubborn negative patterns. Some she thought of were:

+ loyalty to her mother—not wanting to admit Mom was wrong too, not just Dad for picking on her;
+ loyalty to her parents—not wanting to admit that this protracted problem her whole family felt so helpless about might have been solved if it had been tackled constructively instead of with blaming and defending;
+ "magical" thinking—not wanting to give up her illusion that the world will magically be on her side instead of fraught with imaginary dragons like traffic, stoplights, and speed limits;
+ liking the rush of fighting these imaginary dragons.

But as Ellie thought about her life, she decided that the biggest reason she doesn't learn empathy for her husband's feelings is that in the confusing and painful waiting after the accident, no one empathized with her. In Ellie's most traumatic crisis of waiting, no one really saw how afraid she was, so no one showed compassion, said they were sorry, explained what was happening, or helped her pass the time. When no one showed empathy for her, she didn't learn empathy for herself or others either. Instead she told herself that waiting isn't a big deal, that she needed to buck up and stop acting like a baby, and that nothing could be done. And she is still telling herself that waiting isn't a big deal, that her husband should buck up and get used to it, and that it cannot be avoided. She got no empathy for having to wait, so she has no empathy for others. Without this compassion, she is not motivated to change.

Now of course, waiting is inevitable and is not the end of the world, so in one sense Ellie was right about telling herself to buck up. Still, much waiting can be avoided or handled constructively. But Ellie never really admits that waiting is a problem, so she doesn't work at solving it. Instead, she keeps re-creating waiting scenarios for others and then acts dismayed when others don't collude with her belief that waiting is not a big deal. *Or* she admits the problem (but too late to fix it) and then mentally punishes herself for her lateness as her dad would have done.

Last question: What would help me learn this lesson now?

Ellie decided the answer to this question is, "More genuine compassion for myself as a young child having to wait at a frightening accident scene with no one to help me." And, "More problem solving and less blaming around waiting." As she feels empathy for her younger self in that painful time of waiting, she no longer has to pretend that waiting is not a big deal. Instead, she can acknowledge her discomfort, discomfort she does not want to inflict on someone she loves, motivating her to find creative solutions to unnecessary waiting. And when waiting is inevitable, at least she can be genuine in her empathy for others, as she would want them to be with her.

Now it's your turn:

+ When have others done to me what I blame myself for doing? List on the left below as many situations as come to mind.

+ How was I expected to handle each of those situations? List them on the right.

_____	_____
_____	_____
_____	_____
_____	_____
_____	_____

+ What should I have learned in those situations that would help me not repeat them with others? (Include lessons about empathy, yourself, life, and other people, as well as any constructive solutions.)

_____

_____

+ What kept me from learning those lessons? (Examples: a lack of acknowledgment, empathy, or help.)

_____

_____

+ What would help me to learn those lessons now? (Examples: getting from others or yourself the acknowledgment, empathy, or help you needed and did not get.)

_____

_____

Just because Ellie identifies these things does not mean she gets to forgive herself for being late, of course. First she needs to change her behavior, which includes taking sufficient responsibility for being on time, communicating where she is, letting her husband know her plans, and making every effort to follow through on them so he doesn't have to worry any more because she is doing the worrying instead. But at least for now she can forgive herself for one thing: for being blinded by her previous wounds. Once she accepts her blind spots she can begin to compensate for them—to lock up the gun and give away the ammo instead of pretending she can be trusted with them, for starters.

Compassion is the best motivator for lasting change. Compassion stems from really knowing another person and empathizing with his or her experience. It also entails knowing ourselves and empathizing with our own experience so we can heal and change instead of pretending we weren't hurt and aren't hurting anyone else. It is difficult to have compassion for another from the one-down position of a wounded kid desperately looking to others for healing strength. As we empathize with our own pain we begin to grow up—and to take responsibility for not reinflicting similar wounds on others.

Go back to page 83, item #1, for the issue you worked on and rerate the amount of distress you feel about it now. Any better? Worse? If your score has improved substantially, great—this may be all you need to finally forgive yourself. If not, keep reading.

5

REPENTANCE

*I acknowledged my sin unto thee, and mine iniquity have
I not hid. I said, I will confess my transgressions unto the
Lord; and thou forgavest the iniquity of my sin.*

—PSALM 32:5

When we have broken a trust, a law, or a commandment, forgiveness is something we must qualify for—not something we deserve simply because there were mitigating circumstances or we said we were sorry. Qualifying for a race does not mean we deserve to win; it just means we have met the minimal standards to run. When we repent, we meet God's minimal standards for mercy. We can never do enough to deserve to win His forgiveness, but He offers it freely to all who qualify through repentance.

Repentance includes acknowledging our wrongdoing, changing our behavior, confessing our sin, apologizing sincerely, making restitution, earning back violated trust, and learning from our mistakes. It includes accepting legitimate consequences, forgiving others, and demonstrating our sincerity over time. Most important, repentance means acknowledging God's sovereignty in our lives and recommitting to trust Him fully. As we take advantage of all these steps, our commitment to God's laws deepens. We meet the requirements of justice as completely as we can, thereby qualifying for the gift of mercy.

The LDS Bible Dictionary[1] defines repentance as "a change of mind, i.e., a fresh view about God, about oneself, and about the world . . . a turning of the heart and will to God, and a renunciation of sin to which we are naturally inclined." This definition helps clarify that it is possible to change our behavior (e.g., stop swearing) without really repenting or turning our heart to God (e.g., you stop because your boss said you had to). It is also possible to repent (change our mind) before we demonstrate changed behavior. Alma the Younger completely turned his heart to God and was forgiven even before he began his lifetime of service to the Church (Mosiah 27:24). Both a fresh view (changing our mind) and renunciation of sin (changing our behavior and thoughts) indicate true repentance.[2]

CHUTES AND LADDERS

In the childhood game of *Chutes and Ladders*, the playing board has both chutes that take the player down to a previous stage and ladders that shortcut to a higher one. Personal repentance and change can feel like a game of *Chutes and Ladders*, where we make progress only to slip back to where we started, or where "fresh views" about God and ourselves can give us shortcuts to genuine change.[3] I focus this chapter on some of the "chutes" we hit when we're not really clear about such questions as these:

• Have I done something bad enough that I should be apologizing for or changing?

+ Is there hope that I can really change when I have tried before and failed?
+ Is it enough to change my behavior, or do I have to also change my desires?
+ How do I change?
+ How much do I have to change and for how long in order to be forgiven?
+ Is my sin serious enough to involve priesthood leaders or civil authorities?
+ What constitutes a constructive apology, and what do I do if I can't apologize?
+ How do I make restitution, especially if the debt I incurred cannot really be repaid?
+ How do I regain lost trust from other people or myself?
+ If I'm truly sorry, why is God punishing me?
+ What if the other person won't forgive me?
+ In order to be forgiven, do I really have to forgive someone who hurt me even more?
+ What if they hurt me first? Do I still have to repent and forgive?
+ How do I make sense of my life since I've made such big mistakes?
+ How can I know if God has truly forgiven me?

Exploring these questions can help us find ladders to real progress on the path to reconciliation with God, other people, and our own best self.

Have I Done Something Bad Enough That I Should Be Apologizing for or Changing?

Related to this question are such questions as:

+ Is this problem really worth addressing, or is someone else being overly picky about nothing?
+ Is this problem really worth addressing, or am I being overly picky about nothing?

In other words: Am I expecting too much of myself, or not enough? Am I in delusion about my sin, or do I have healthy self-acceptance of my weakness?

When looking back on my life, I can forget that misdeeds in my life's rearview mirror may be closer (or farther away) than they appear. I overreact to some of my errors and underreact to others, even when I am sincere and prayerful. *The Spirit will surely guide me in such matters.* But sometimes the Spirit first expects me to work on my own to figure these things out. *Other people can help me get a truer perspective about whether I'm being overly nonchalant or overly self-critical.*

Of course, we are trying to distinguish thoughtlessness, forgetfulness, or other mortal weakness from sin. I may offend my father by forgetting his birthday, but that doesn't really qualify as a serious sin against God. I may need to work at being more thoughtful of other people, but I don't necessarily need to label myself an uncharitable ingrate or invest in a complete personality overhaul.

As we make such distinctions, it also helps to *separate events from patterns.* If I forgot my father's birthday this year, I probably need to apologize, try to make it up to him, and let it go. If I forget everyone's birthday for three months running, I may need to take a look at my life to see if perhaps I need more household help, better time-management skills, or treatment for depression. If I remember everyone's birthday except my dad's and I forget it every year, perhaps I'm carrying a grudge that needs repentance and healing so I don't keep acting it out in this less-than-honest manner.

I can also look at overall patterns in whether I ignore problems or exaggerate them. I've probably gotten messages from many people about whether I tend to overemphasize others' faults or my own, and what things I almost always brush off versus what kinds of molehills I make into mountains. Awareness of such patterns can help me decide if a particular offense I've committed needs to be taken more or less seriously than I am inclined to take it.

Even if what I've done wrong is the moral equivalent of stepping on an ant, my behavior is a big problem for the ant. If I hurt someone else, especially someone close to me, apologies and change may be in order even if I don't think I violated a major law of God or country. If the person I offended is especially sensitive to a certain kind of mishap on my part, but I keep mishapping anyway, then my weakness may become a stumbling block for another that true charity demands I try harder to change. At minimum, integrity may require that I explain why I don't think their request is reasonable, complete with both careful listening and calm, honest words.

If my partner or child is a decent person but ignores my efforts to negotiate, perhaps I have gotten into a habit of criticism and complaints they block out to safeguard their sanity. I may need to work on reducing my criticism rather than fixing my loved one. Conversely, if my spouse brings up problems but I never do, perhaps I don't really invest in the relationship or am too preoccupied with other things to care what happens at home. Passively ignoring issues until they blow up can be as damaging as constant criticism.

If a particular problem behavior is not near the top of my own change priority list, my housemates' change priority list for me, or

God's change priority list, it is probably okay to tackle things that are more pressing first and remind myself *that I can handle only so much self-improvement at once.*

Is There Hope That I Can Really Change When I Have Tried Before and Failed?

The simple answer is yes! Don't we all know someone who has successfully quit smoking or lost weight after several failed attempts? In fact, *research indicates that most people who succeed at a big change have failed several times first.* Each failure is an opportunity to improve our chances of success the next time—if we analyze what happened, learn from our mistakes, and try something new.[4]

Unfortunately, many of us don't go to this effort. Instead, we blame ourselves or someone else as sinful and perhaps punish ourselves with self-loathing but don't really try a new approach. We assume we are failing to repent (and so must just be incorrigible) instead of failing at a normal mortal weakness that calls for deeper humility, careful prioritizing of our effort, building on our strengths, and improving over time. We either give up completely or keep trying the same ineffective approaches with little thought and then wonder why we don't succeed. But if we do not understand at a pretty deep level why we do what we do, what events trigger our bad choices, our resources and options, and the benefits of change, chances are we will not improve.

In fact, *until we really "get" the prices we are paying for our poor choices and the superior benefits we stand to gain from finding another way, research suggests that we may be better off not trying to change.*[5] Like the foolish man who does not count the cost before starting his building project (Luke 14:28–30), we will probably run out of steam long before completion, leaving us more convinced than ever that lasting change is impossible.

A better approach is to gather motivation first by

+ studying the issue,
+ making a list of the pros and cons of change,
+ reading those articles in the *Ensign* and elsewhere that we prefer to ignore because they make us feel guilty,
+ talking with people who have succeeded where we have failed.

Keep a running list of the advantages and disadvantages of change, and work to make the advantages list long and personally meaningful before you begin. Try to neutralize some of the disadvantages of change and strengthen the advantages until you are convinced that change is worthwhile for you. Changing your mind precedes changing your behavior.[6]

Is It Enough to Change My Behavior, or Do I Have to Also Change My Desires?

This question comes up a lot for people struggling with addictions like drugs or sex, or deep-seated predispositions like obsessive-compulsive disorder or same-gender attraction. While we want to change our very desire for sin, *we won't necessarily stop wanting wrong things altogether; we will just desire God more.* My body will always want food on fast Sunday, but my desire to fast can be firm. I may always feel the impulse to yell at my kids when angry, but I can desire more to be a calm, patient parent. A tempting thought or feeling does not make me a bad person—even Christ was tempted in all things (Hebrews 4:15). We want to retrain ourselves not to see temptation as a cue to act out but as a prompt to seek support, manage stress better, change our environment, exercise more, lose ourselves in service, pay attention to relationships, or have a good laugh. In the war against temptation, distraction and self-care are much better weapons than self-preoccupation and self-hatred.

A man who struggled for years with a sexual addiction before getting "sober" was asked by someone still in the throes of addiction, "Do you ever get to a place where these things no longer tempt you, or do you just get better at resisting?" He answered thoughtfully, "I am still tempted at times, but now instead of seeing temptation as something I will eventually and inevitably give in to, I see temptation as a cue that I need more meaningful time with friends, support for my self-esteem, better stress management at work, or connection with people who really know and love me. *I'm more likely to tempt myself with my old addiction when I'm not taking care of myself,* and I am learning to see such temptations as an indicator that I need to pay more attention to what is missing in my life and discover how to fix it rather than seeing temptation as my cue to act out. White-knuckle resistance and giving in are not the only choices."

But what about temptations that take the form of thoughts more than behavior, like pride, jealousy, or doubt? How much must I change these thoughts and feelings in order to repent? Is a prideful thought a temptation to be ignored or a reflection of my character and worldview that I need to tackle and dismantle? Even in these cases, gently evoking feelings of humility, self-worth, and trust in God may be a better strategy than berating or labeling ourselves. Deciding that a prideful thought is a temptation I will choose to ignore demonstrates my highest values.

How Do I Change?

We've noted two broad categories of personal change in the scriptures. In one situation the person sins, willfully blind to his behavior and its consequences because of self-deception or the deception of others. Once his eyes are opened to see his sin for what it is, his change of heart can be dramatic and complete. Alma the Younger (Mosiah 27), King Lamoni (Alma 18), and Saul on the road to Damascus (Acts 9) are examples. Willful disobedience to God is sin.

In the second situation, misdeeds reflect weakness rather than sin—weakness such as immaturity at handling life's challenges, a need for gradual growth and improvement, common fears and insecurities, or inaccurate maps of how life works. This kind of change is more likely to come over time and require persistent effort, help and support from others, careful self-observation and reflection, and taking the risks of a new approach. Examples are Peter's gradual maturing as a leader, Joseph Smith's lengthy tutoring in obedience, or Moses's emerging victory over his fear of Pharaoh.

Even with the category of sin, sometimes a fresh view that allows us to see where we have been blind and deceived will help us change more than will an exhaustive system of rewards or punishments for our behavior. Even with weakness, seeing where we have been blind and deceived may lead to "aha!" moments that facilitate big, lasting change. We can make more room for such occasions by asking God and other people to show us where we are missing some essential self-understanding—and then believing them.

Renunciation of sin may also require a gradual reshaping of habits, insecurities, fears, and maps. We must choose again and again those things we trust will work in the long run, not looking for some quick fix to eliminate struggles or hard choices. While being confronted by an angel on the roadside may make our choices clearer, true *Christian discipleship will always require sacrifice, effort, and facing down our fears.*

Thus planning becomes an important step in most change, and

that means identifying when the problem comes up (times, places, and relationships), what triggers our bad choices (self-talk, reminders of old pain, insecurities, hunger, or fatigue), making a concrete plan for what we will do instead (including changes in our environment, thinking, and self-care), and especially planning for how we will get ourselves back on track when we slip (calling a friend, having a ritual of renewed effort, examining and learning from setbacks). *Most of us need more information before we ever start a change process*—information about why change will bless us, how others have tackled this problem, what personal insecurities feed our bad behavior, and what resources are available to support our efforts to change. "Going public," asking for support, removing temptations if possible, and praying about our decisions will help us succeed.

Deciding up front what we will do when we slip is invaluable because we probably will slip. *Making a plan for handling slips is not a sign that we aren't serious about changing—it is a way to say we are so serious about changing that even a slip will not derail us.* Setbacks do not mean it is time to give up but time to be more honest, ask for help, apologize, analyze what went wrong, and start again.

Sometimes *big changes in our lives begin with small steps in the right direction.*[7] Playing different music, taking a walk after dinner, calling a friend once a week, or keeping a journal may feel like inadequate tools for reshaping my personality, but sometimes by such "small and simple things are great things brought to pass" (Alma 37:6).

How Much Do I Have to Change and for How Long to Be Forgiven?

We've talked about two broad categories, sin and weakness, with the line demarcating them being fuzzy. Among the big-ticket sins are sexual misconduct, violence, child abuse or neglect, abortion, apostasy, cheating, lying, murder,[8] stealing, drug abuse—things people get arrested for or that threaten Church membership. These sins carry big price tags, and we know they gravely damage ourselves and others. When dealing with big-ticket sins, we generally know at some level that we have serious work to do, even if we have rationalized our behavior. *Spiritual progress is almost impossible until we take care of our big-ticket sins.* The goal is complete elimination of these sins forever. When we eliminate such a sin for a long enough time that our bishop, spouse, probation officer, or employer writes us a clean bill of health, we can anticipate God's forgiveness as well. If we repeat the sin we will have to start over; then trust will take longer to restore, the consequences will be higher, and forgiveness will take longer.

Then there is the endless-list category of sin or weakness that we still know is wrong, but we are less clear exactly how wrong. These are both sins and weaknesses of omission and commission that range from taking pencils from work to gossiping about our neighbors, from yelling at our kids to neglecting our family history research, from shopping on Sunday to neglecting to pray. Some of these behaviors are still quite serious and others almost trivial. We have so many of these floating around in our lives that we are hard-pressed to know which ones are most important to address, which ones are really sins, and which ones are just annoying weaknesses— or how much others have the right to push us to change them.

We will probably never get to the bottom of the endless list, but the more spiritual we are the more of these we tend to notice, feel guilt for, and desire to work on. But priorities will vary widely from person to person and even culture to culture on which ones are most pressing. Some of these are more clearly sins to eliminate (cheating on taxes), others are weaknesses to reduce (whining and pouting), others are positive behaviors to work on (attending the temple more), and still others we may never get around to. Overcoming endless-list sins and weaknesses presents a great opportunity for ongoing improvement, practice in balancing and prioritizing, and being "anxiously engaged in a good cause, [to] do many good things of [our] own free will, and bring to pass much righteousness" (D&C 58:27). These sins and weaknesses are definitely worth attending to and working on. But they also may require goals of *progress and balance more than absolute, always/never obedience.*

Is My Sin Serious Enough to Involve Priesthood Leaders or Civil Authorities?

Quite simply, big-ticket sins are serious matters that disrupt society and families and can seriously damage innocent people. If we are involved in a big-ticket sin, *we need support and help in changing, including the support that comes from facing the consequences of our choices.* Facing consequences helps us take our sins more seriously and gives us added motivation for change. It also helps those we hurt and betray to know they have not had to suffer for our bad choices while we've gone free, and that they are not crazy to think what we did was wrong. When we submit voluntarily to rehab, Church disciplinary councils, or civil law, we allow our freedoms to be restricted so that (among other reasons) those we've hurt can begin to feel freer and safer again.

Research suggests that women who confessed sexual misconduct to a bishop and were not invited to pay a reasonable price often felt they and their sins were not being taken seriously.[9] While Church leaders should rightfully be kind and supportive of anyone seeking their help, a period of soul-searching, restriction of Church involvement, and making restitution generally helps us know we have paid a price for our choices and can therefore stop waiting for the other shoe to fall. Paying a price helps both reinforce and satisfy our appropriate sense of justice.

What Constitutes a Constructive Apology, and What Do I Do If I Can't Apologize?

While many people will accept a clear effort to change as sufficient, apologizing as well is like signing a peace treaty, not just withdrawing troops. Apologizing makes our intentions and values clear. *Sincere apologies must be followed by real change*, and if we don't intend to change we should not bother to apologize, since doing so will only undermine trust. Apologizing for every little thing until people get sick of it is no better. Sincere apologies do not have to include groveling self-condemnation, nor should they include a commensurate list of the other person's faults. A heartfelt apology simply acknowledges that we did something hurtful, that we feel bad about it, that we want to make it right, and that we intend to do better in the future. The scriptures encourage wrongdoers to "return unto [those we hurt], and acknowledge your faults and that wrong which ye have done" (Alma 39:13).

We may struggle with apologies if we have experienced major injuries for which no one has apologized to us. We may also struggle to apologize if we have never really seen it done, or if we have gotten the message that admitting a mistake is a sign of weakness instead of a sign of strength. Apologizing is also hard if the other person never seems satisfied with our apologies, although this can indicate that we are missing an aspect of apology that matters to the other person but not to us (like admitting wrongdoing or expressing empathy for the other's feelings). Knowing the different ways other people judge the sincerity of an apology can help us apologize more effectively. Elements of a sincere apology usually include:

+ A simple acknowledgment of what we did wrong and that we know it was wrong
+ Empathy and sorrow for the other person's hurt or angry feelings
+ A statement about what we would like to do to try to make it up to the person
+ An explanation of what we intend to do to change and to rebuild their trust
+ A request for forgiveness[10]

Occasionally our efforts to apologize are unsuccessful. If we find our apology falling on deaf ears, we may have omitted an element that happens to be very important to the other person and without which the person doesn't believe an apology is sincere. People may also reject our apology if we have a history of apologizing without changing, or if they think we are invasive, insensitive, or inappropriate. Sometimes they feel too hurt at the moment and need time to regroup, or they need to first see that we will put our money where our mouth is by really changing.

How Do I Make Restitution, Especially If the Debt I Incurred Cannot Really Be Repaid?

I once had a client come to ask for help with self-forgiveness. He had abused a former employer's trust by giving huge, unwarranted discounts to his friends. He was a sincere, spiritual young man who had gone to his bishop and had been told to stop worrying. After all, he was young when this happened, his employer had long since moved away, and there was no real way to repay what had been taken. Liking this young man and wanting him to put this much-regretted incident behind him, I reiterated the bishop's advice. But looking back I feel we both did this wonderful young man a great disservice by not helping him figure out how to make restitution for his dishonesty, or connect his current good choices to the repayment of that debt. He carried the burden of his mistake much too long because we did not uphold his conscience and values by helping him make up for his wrongdoing.

Twelve-step programs that help people overcome addictions all include taking a sincere accounting of one's wrongdoings and making sincere efforts to right all old wrongs. Most participants in these programs find this one of the most difficult—and freeing—steps in their recovery. All of us can benefit from this step. We can write a letter of apology stating what we did wrong, what we learned, and what we will do to try to pay the person back. If we can't do everything at once, we can propose a payment schedule or suggest an alternative restitution. If we took far more than we can ever repay, we can at least make a serious effort that costs us something close to what we cost the other person.

Restitution requires some creativity if the person we harmed is no longer available to receive our restitution. *If we cannot pay the person back directly or completely, we can estimate the damage we did and do as much as we can to make it right.* The young man above did not know how to locate his former employer, but he could have donated a reasonable sum to charity or volunteered equivalent time to a good cause. He could tutor for free, coach a team, or clean up a campsite on his own time. He could give talks to local businesses on how to prevent employee theft, create a job for a young person in need, or help support a missionary. Such acts, when done as an offering of restitution to God and society, can help us complete our repentance.

Sometimes the only restitution we can make is to try to understand what circumstances in our lives led us to the sin we committed and to do all we can to *correct those circumstances for others* (for example, be a good parent, fight poverty, teach by example, and so forth). The scriptures speak of the sons of Mosiah making restitution by "zealously striving to repair all the injuries which they had done to the church, confessing all their sins, and publishing all the things which they had seen, and explaining the prophecies and the scriptures to all who desired to hear them" (Mosiah 27:35). This falls under Elder Neal A. Maxwell's counsel: "Sometimes . . . restitution is not possible in real terms, such as when one contributed to another's loss of faith or virtue. Instead, a subsequent example of righteousness provides a compensatory form of restitution."[11]

How Do I Regain Lost Trust from Other People or Myself?

The onus is on us to restore a broken trust, not on the other person to just decide to trust us. We can present our plan for how we intend to be more honest, thoughtful, or faithful in the future, ask if the plan makes sense to the other person or if the person would like us to take other steps, and then do all we can to be open and above board. We should not submit to cruel or unusual punishment. But we do need to realize that rebuilding trust takes time and is not owed us just because we are sorry.

As much as the other person doesn't want to be hurt by us again, trust is not rebuilt by pretending we are never tempted, but by showing the other person how we handle temptation. A client who had had a serious problem with pornography thought his wife would be horrified if she knew he still was tempted by his old habits. He reassured her constantly that pornography would never be an issue for him again. As much as she wanted to believe him, she was doubtful. He did not regain her trust by hiding his problem so she would not have to worry but by being honest about his problem so they could work together to overcome it. When he was honest about times when he was tempted but also told her what he had done to stay clean, she began to trust that he really was making progress. *We don't regain others' trust by assuring them there is nothing to worry about but by showing that we are doing the worrying for them so they don't have to.*

Trusting ourselves again also takes time. Trust increases as we come to understand what made us vulnerable to sin, how much we hurt those whose trust we violated, and what we need to do to avoid and resist temptation. *Making a list of things we are learning* helps us see our progress in understanding what went wrong and making needed change.

If I'm Truly Sorry, Why Is God Punishing Me?

Adam and Eve repented for yielding to temptation in the garden, but they were still evicted from Eden and they still died, just as God had forewarned (D&C 29:40–42; Moses 6:52–53). *Because God's laws are descriptions of reality, not arbitrary pronouncements, real consequences follow the options He forbids.* True, not all of these consequences always follow (sexual promiscuity does not always lead to disease or pregnancy), but life does not owe us a reprieve. If consequences could always be averted, then we would have little reason to take God's descriptions seriously. He would essentially be lying to us about what is real, which He will not do. Accepting the consequences of our choices is part of how we yield to God's sovereignty, trusting *that if we are repentant He can still forgive and bless us, even if He cannot always protect us.*

What If the Other Person Won't Forgive Me?

Some people have a harder time forgiving than others. If I knock someone down who already has a broken leg, it may take a lot longer for him to recover than for someone who can jump back up and laugh off my clumsiness. This just comes with the territory of hurting other people. Sometimes we just have to patiently wait for another's forgiveness. But *sometimes we can ease the process.* A checklist to consider:

- Have I apologized in a way that honors and acknowledges the person's pain, not just mine?
- Have I said exactly what I did that was wrong, and does the other person agree?
- Have I listened with empathy and without defensiveness to what the person is feeling?
- Have I made restitution?
- Have I asked if there is more the person needs from me and honestly tried to give it?
- Have I changed the behavior that hurt the person?
- Have I given the person time, or am I more interested in my comfort?
- Have I asked for forgiveness?

If we have done our part, we can still forgive ourselves and move on without bitterness while we allow the other person his own feelings. The other person doesn't have to agree that we deserve forgiveness for us to let go.

What If They Hurt Me First?
Do I Still Have to Repent and Forgive?

Of course they hurt you first—why else would you have done what you did? You aren't just a bully or a monster—you have good reasons for lashing out, or being defensive, or trying to get them to see how unfair and selfish they are being. Even if *this* person didn't really do much to hurt you first, *someone* has hurt you first, leaving you with an axe to grind and a wound to lick. *God's commandments to repent and to forgive others are not just for the unwounded.* Even when we get hurt first, forgiveness helps put us back in control of our lives and stop the progression of retaliation and repetition.

This does not suggest that our hurts do not also deserve attention and restitution. It just means we are not stuck waiting for others to see the light and repent in order for us to see the light and repent. When my colleagues and I offer seminar retreats on forgiving others, most people come in bleeding with anger and frustration, wondering how they can ever get their sister, brother, spouse, parent, child, boss, or neighbor to finally stop acting like a jerk so peace and harmony can finally be restored. After a day of hard work, these same people often walk out feeling hope, healing, and a measure of peace—even though the person who hurt them has not changed an iota. One of the great messages of Jesus Christ was that the Jews didn't have to wait for liberation from the Romans to find freedom, they didn't have to wait for the Pharisees to stop bickering to find peace, and they didn't have to wait for their friends and family to convert to live the gospel themselves. We can feel resentful when the Spirit points out our faults when we think we are only reacting to the stupidity or bullheadedness of another. God's hard truths will help us solve our problems and get moving again; waiting for others to change may not.

We also need empathy for ourselves, not only for those we hurt. As we more fully understand the hurts or fears that led us to a bad choice, we need compassion for the blind and frightened part of us that hides behind our show of toughness or indifference, or that cowers in self-pity or self-blame. Someone has said that to understand all is to forgive all. While this is not always true, we have also been hurt, and we also deserve our empathy and understanding.

Forgiving others is not something we just naturally know how to do or something that happens just because we decide it should. People who study forgiveness say it is a process with predictable steps.[12] I believe these steps follow scriptural laws of justice and mercy. Unless the other person is willing to participate in that process with us, the kind of forgiving we can experience is limited and may not include reconciliation or improved mutual understanding. But we can still claim many of the blessings forgiving affords.

Forgiving others does not require us to claim that no harm was done—that we were not really hurt after all. Forgiving does not mean we must admit they were right and we were wrong. It does not require us to reconcile or reestablish a relationship with someone who is dangerous or uncaring. It does not require us to forget what happened and erase it from our memory banks. It does not excuse the other person from the legal consequences of his actions.

Forgiving others does allow us to lay claim on Christ for what was taken from us. It does allow us to stop feeling like a powerless victim and regain a sense of equality and strength, as well as compassion. It does mean we choose to grow and move on instead of being caught in the web of old injuries. It does mean we act to protect ourselves and those we love from further harm. It does mean we choose kindness and compassion over bitterness and vengeance.

When we walk the road toward forgiving others, we meet God coming toward us.

How Do I Make Sense of My Life Since I've Made Such Big Mistakes?

Seventeenth-century philosopher Baruch de Spinoza counsels: "Do not weep; do not wax indignant. Understand."[13] This life philosophy is a powerful antidote to self-pity, even when our sins fill us with remorse or leave us wondering why God did not stop us from doing *that*. Our task when we sin is not to turn back the clock or metamorphose into an angel or, barring such magic, to dissolve into despair. Our task is to learn. To learn to see where we have been blind. To learn to transcend evil. To learn the humility and charity of God. To learn.

"What have I learned?" is a question that helps me go forward when I want to sit down and mope about my failures. Make a list of what you have learned, and the fog lifts a bit, the pathway forward reemerges. This is not to say that our sins are really okay because, after all, look at all we learned. But it is to say that *if we have to pay the price of shame, guilt, consequences, and hurting those we love, then at least let's not miss the lessons.* Even if we do not feel we learned enough to be worth what we and others paid, Christ is willing to repay our losses if we consecrate both the pain and the learning to Him. The principle of consecration says that as we put everything on the altar, and I think this includes even our sins, He will give us back what is for our good. As we let these lessons permeate our art, our work, our relationships, and our service, we work with God to make new life out of spilt blood.

How Can I Know If God Has Truly Forgiven Me?

Church leaders can help us know. Prayer can help us know. Scriptures can help us know. The forgiveness of those we injured can help us know. Our emotions alone do *not* always help us know because we too readily assume lack of guilt means all is well or that still feeling bad means we're not forgiven. People in the boxes of Delusion, Despair, or Distrust can't always trust their emotions to tell them the truth. God, however, will. *Our task is not to somehow stop finding our sins abhorrent but to find joy in our redemption.*

Once we have taken the steps of repentance, we have the

privilege "not to fear, but with penitence to ask [God's] forgiveness in full confidence of receiving it."[14] That assurance of forgiveness may not come as a dramatic event or a wildly joyful feeling but as a quiet, accumulating witness that we are doing what we can, that God loves us and is pleased with our progress, and that there is hope. Sometimes the Spirit will whisper about steps we yet need to take to obtain the forgiveness we seek. But when we repent, the promise of God's eventual forgiveness is sure.

Of course, continued self-flagellation is a choice but not usually a helpful one (see chapter 8). As we see ourselves choosing to dwell on our failures, we can decide to choose something else instead—something like belief in Christ, gratitude for His atonement, and reinvestment in life. In trying to decide if the internal voice reminding me of my failures is God's voice, Satan's, or just my own regret, I have learned a crucial lesson: *God doesn't yell.* If the voice in my head is belittling, hopeless, name-calling, sarcastic, mean-spirited, mocking, scornful, or indifferent, it is not God talking (Nehemiah 9:17). I can choose to believe this disparaging voice if I want, but if I do it will really be a choice to believe Satan or myself or my third-grade teacher, who is still rattling around in my memory tapes—not a choice to believe God.

FINAL CONSIDERATIONS

King Benjamin counsels his people in the Book of Mormon:

> Consider on the blessed and happy state of those that keep the commandments of God. For behold, they are blessed in all things, both temporal and spiritual; and if they hold out faithful to the end they are received into heaven, that thereby they may dwell with God in a state of

never-ending happiness. O remember, remember that these things are true; for the Lord God hath spoken it (Mosiah 2:41).

Ah, yes, I may sigh, consider those blessed and happy people who are so much better than I, who do the right things, who aren't proud or angry or insensitive or weak, who obey the commandments and deserve to be happy. But what is the most often-repeated commandment of God? It is not to be perfect, charitable, disciplined, calm, or right. It is to repent. I may not be good at perfection, but even *I* can get good at repenting. As I do I can yet qualify for this "blessed and happy state" of the obedient. *I will never overcome all my weaknesses in this life, but I can repent of all my sins.* I can be blameless before God if I repent.

Jesus not only has the desire and will to save us because of His great love; He has also earned the *right* to be merciful to us through His atonement. He can "claim of the Father his rights of mercy which he hath upon the children of men. . . . For he hath answered the ends of the law, and he claimeth all those who have faith in him; and they who have faith in him will cleave unto every good thing; wherefore he advocateth the cause of the children of men" (Moroni 7:27–28). He can extend His rights of mercy to us without violating the demands of justice if we have faith in Him and repent.

Grace bridges the gap between our sincere but always inadequate repentance and the demands of justice. We can never do enough to earn forgiveness—it is a gift we can never fully merit. Yet we can still be "perfect in Christ" and "sanctified in Christ by the grace of God, through the shedding of the blood of Christ . . . unto the remission of [our] sins, that [we] may become holy, without spot" as we "deny [ourselves] of all ungodliness [sin], and love God with all [our] might, mind and strength" (Moroni 10:32–33).

We can know that He forgives us if we repent for the same

reason that the brother of Jared claimed his redemption—because we believe that God is a God of truth and cannot lie (Ether 3:11–14). He has promised again and again to forgive the penitent (see, for example, Isaiah 1:18; Jeremiah 32:8; Micah 7:18–19; Acts 13:38–39; Hebrews 8:12; Moroni 6:8; D&C 1:32; 58:42). His promise is neatly summarized in the words, "Yea, and as often as my people repent will I forgive them their trespasses against me" (Mosiah 26:30).

God always keeps His promises.

SUMMARY

As you review the issue you identified in this chapter, what aspects of this issue suggest sins of rebellion or disobedience for which repentance is warranted? What aspects of this issue represent weakness associated with being a fallible, limited mortal?

Which of the steps of repentance for sin still need attention:

☐ I need to do more to change my heart by seeing the extent of the harm I've caused or by trusting more deeply in God's description of reality. I could do this by: _____

_____

☐ I need to do more to change my behavior, specifically:

_____

☐ I need to do more to apologize, focusing on the following aspects of an effective apology: _____

_____

☐ I need to do more to make restitution, which I could do by:_____

_____

Which of the steps of humility for weakness still need attention:

☐ I need to prioritize which weakness I will work on now:

☐ I need to do more to learn more about the following issues related to my weakness: _____

_____

☐ I need to practice or be more patient with the following:

_____

_____

☐ I need to build on my strengths of:_____

_____

☐ I need contingency plans for getting back on track, such as: _____

PART 3

OVERCOMING INTERNAL OBSTACLES TO PEACE

When we don't forgive ourselves, we get stuck in the boxes of Delusion, Despair, and Distrust. This section of the book considers some of the personality styles and life experiences that can make it difficult to trust that God's forgiveness applies to us personally. Chapters 6 to 10 will explore the hidden, erroneous assumptions behind shame and pride (delusion/despair), depression (despair), anxious perfectionism (distrust), self-destructive unselfishness (distrust), and trauma and abuse (distrust). Some of these assumptions apply to most of us at least some of the time and can block our progress toward self-forgiveness (for sin) and self-acceptance (for weakness).

Remember that self-forgiveness is "trust that God's gift of forgiveness applies to my sin." Self-forgiveness after repentance for sin is different from self-acceptance after humbly acknowledging our weakness.

Self-forgiveness and self-acceptance are one position among several possibilities, described as follows:

		UNREPENTANT OR NO GROWTH	REPENTANCE OR MUCH GROWTH
SELF-ASSESSMENT	POSITIVE	Delusion	Self-Forgiveness/ Self-Acceptance
	NEGATIVE	Despair	Distrust
		REPENTANCE OR HUMILITY	

Diagram 3: Responses to Sin or Weakness

Delusion suggests that I see no need to repent or change, even though I sin or am weak.

Despair suggests that I see no possibility of real change, but I know I need it.

Distrust suggests that I have repented or grown, but I don't forgive or accept myself.

In the chapters that follow, we'll consider some common personality styles that get in the way of Self-Forgiveness and Self-Acceptance. Whether or not you exhibit this style most of the time, some of the assumptions and thought patterns of this style may sound familiar, especially when you are being hard on yourself. Seeing how psychologists help people with these styles to grow and heal can help us move out of Delusion, Despair, and Distrust toward Self-Forgiveness and Self-Acceptance.

6

SHAME AND PRIDE

Our dignity as human beings, paradoxically, depends
upon the acceptance of our shame.

—FREDERICK TURNER[1]

Teeter-totters are a standard item on playgrounds, to the delight of children everywhere. It is a dazzling experience to fly into the air on the momentum of another person's plunge to the ground and then to wait precariously at the pinnacle of our glory to plummet down again. We are never so perfectly balanced against our partner in play that a little jiggling can't offset us; then a mighty push sends us heavenward again. But we can soar only if someone else is anchoring the other side of the plank, bottoming out as we fly up. And our turn at the bottom will inevitably follow every temporary victory over the laws of gravity.

Many of us live on a teeter-totter that follows similar rules but is not nearly as much fun. It is the teeter-totter of basing our self-image on the illusion of superiority. On this teeter-totter, self-esteem comes from staying in the air, possible only if someone else is lower than we are. Yet the threat of our own fall from grace is always present. We are either riding high on pride or scraping bottom in shame. When we fall we feel like frauds, exposed for our "real" worthlessness. But even when we rise we know that we will descend in only a matter of time.

Forgiving ourselves is hard when we live on the teeter-totter of shame and pride. To forgive ourselves requires first accepting our failings and repenting; yet if such admissions leave us plummeting to the ground, feeling hopelessly irrelevant and inferior as others soar heavenward, who will have the courage to confess an error? We struggle instead to push out of our lowly state and to leverage ourselves upward through success, achievement, and denial of fault. We ignore reminders that gravity applies to us as well as to others. We bolster our pride when riding high, and we sink into shame when someone else is smarter, stronger, more talented, or more powerful. We aren't necessarily enjoying the ride, but we really don't know how to get off the teeter-totter of superiority-based worth. We cling to Delusion, perhaps periodically plummet into Despair, but never get to the quadrant of real Self-Forgiveness or Self-Acceptance.

LIFE ON THE TEETER-TOTTER

Some people have a tendency toward excessive shame that is evident to those around them, as if they knew no other place in life than holding down the bottom of the teeter-totter so others could soar. Other people cover feelings of shame with boasting, needing to be right, or preoccupation with self, but shame is still at the heart of their behavior. Such folks don't necessarily look utterly self-centered to others—in fact, they may appear outwardly caring or kind—but inside they are boosting their self-esteem with an excessive focus on being right and looking like the superior people they secretly fear they are not. They may appear to be flying high, may look and feel confident much of the time, but may chafe under any criticism, get overly annoyed if things don't go their way, or assume they should not have to endure inconveniences lesser mortals must endure. They believe that their worth is defined by superiority to others and that only displays of accomplishment and others' admiration stand between them and feeling utterly insignificant.

Just as shame underlies what looks like overconfidence, pride can underlie what looks like deep humility for people on the teeter-totter. When we think we have done a merely mediocre job, we may be sure others are disappointed or even embarrassed for us. Our own excessive shame at anything less than a dazzling display is a sneaky form of pride—a way to hold on to the illusion that we should be above the ordinary, and that if we are not exceptional others will have no reason to like or admire us any more. Being just a little better than others is the only way to keep our distance from feelings of not really measuring up. Life on the teeter-totter can be tough.

Ironically, some people on the teeter-totter may not make much effort to excel. They get the strokes they crave only if they are able to pull off their accomplishments by dazzling talent—being lighter than air—rather than by serious effort. Others work very hard to achieve and then feel like frauds because they were not smart enough to get to the top on talent alone. For both groups, being criticized or admitting error can result in a drop in self-esteem so severe that it threatens to undermine their entire self-image. Instead of mistakes prompting learning and growth, errors can feel so shameful as to virtually preclude acknowledgment, humility, learning, and self-acceptance. Sins can be even harder to admit, repent of, and then forgive. It is hard to get to self-forgiveness when just the first step of repentance—admitting fault—makes a person feel ashamed and inferior. When we see ourselves as inherently flawed, foolish, or inferior unless admired and approved, criticism or correction are bitter pills.

Steve is the bane of his college intramural basketball team. He is a reasonably good shooter, and his self-esteem is boosted when he makes his shot, so when he gets the ball he generally shoots. He is vaguely aware that others get annoyed with him but he is not sure why, so he tries to prove his value by getting more points. He doesn't realize that this actually irritates his teammates, who wish he would also pass the ball and play defense. Even his own teammates get tired of him never admitting his fouls. His sense of self-worth comes from making points, never being wrong, and being so invaluable that he doesn't have to do dirty work. Every basket is vindication of his worth and every miss undermines it, leaving him on the bottom of the teeter-totter and fighting to regain position by scoring.

Although Steve really has a good heart, he is too preoccupied with his own needs to have room for much interest in others. He doesn't like to try new things for fear of looking foolish. He talks with feeling about the poor in third-world countries, but his siblings and roommates feel ignored. He idolizes his fiancée and can hardly believe how beautiful and loving she is, but sometimes she really disappoints him with her shallow intellect and lack of athleticism. His tendencies to overidealize and then be disappointed in himself also show up with her. He also feels jealous and angry when his own family seems to prefer her to him. Steve spends a lot of time trying to get to the top of the teeter-totter, feeling hurt when others seem to want to pull him down.

Amy, on the other hand, is accomplished and charismatic and knows how to work a crowd. She is admired and sought out by others because she always has an interesting story to tell and can be counted on to help someone out or offer good advice. She loves learning new crafts and technologies that allow her to excel quickly. Although people find Amy a little intimidating, they feel special and chosen when they are close to her. After a while they start to notice the subtle ways she promotes herself, surrounding herself with people whose problems make her own life look charmed. Her children are always exceptional, her projects are always fascinating; even her problems seem more important and captivating than other people's. But no one ever really feels close to her. She lives her life on one end of the teeter-totter and can keep her place only if she keeps others at a distance.

We don't have to be as self-conscious as Steve or as outwardly dazzling as Amy to have taken a few turns on the teeter-totter of shame and pride. Whenever we look with envy on another's gifts while doubting our own, we are on the teeter-totter. Whenever we are defensive about our mistakes because admitting them fills us with shame, we are on the teeter-totter. Whenever we try to keep others at a distance so they won't pierce our veneer of accomplishment and see our real foibles, we are on the teeter-totter. And life on the teeter-totter is rarely graced with genuine self-forgiveness.

HOW DID WE GET HERE?

How do we end up on the teeter-totter of shame and pride? When children receive praise for outstanding traits but excessive criticism for normal human weakness, they are not really seen for the whole of who they are. They may conclude that they matter only for their gifts and accomplishments and end up feeling deeply ashamed of even normal laziness, messiness, mediocrity, or fears. Parents who show excessive pride in accomplishments but shame or blame children for limitations or weakness strap their kids to teeter-totters of shame and pride. We remember that Heavenly Father delights in our gifts and goodness but offers grace (help, comfort, acceptance, and patience) with our weakness, which He acknowledges as not only inevitable but also valuable.

While parents naturally enjoy their children's unique talents and traits, *if a child's accomplishments become fodder for a parent's ego, children feel used.* The children will learn to feel ashamed of the weaknesses and failings that are the flip sides of all gifts and accomplishments. Their good qualities or accomplishments must be large enough to sustain feelings of superiority (not mere achievement), without which they may feel like nothing. Error must be defended against because it means one is hopelessly defective and unlovable, not just human and in process.

Both highs and lows are part of every mortal life, and the momentum created by moments of difficulty and pain can enrich our lives with empathy for others, problems to solve, and appreciation for our blessings. But on the teeter-totter, difficulties are evidence that we are no longer special and favored, so all of our energy goes into staying up, even at the expense of others. We know we feel bad when others look more important or talented, but the only solution we can imagine is to jump higher or push them lower. The idea of simply getting off the teeter-totter does not even register.

On the teeter-totter, it is hard to imagine finding a sense of worth in the simple integrity of exploring all our feelings, letting ourselves be known without feeling ashamed, and being genuinely interested in and moved by other people. Solving problems or tackling challenges for the sheer satisfaction of engaging life and developing our skills is foreign. We think it is nice that God cares about the orphans, the poor, the sick, and the blind, but we can't really imagine that He doesn't prefer the polished, the capable, the lovely, and the strong.

One of the challenges I face in writing this chapter is that no one really wants to see himself as a self-centered, uncaring person blind to his own preoccupation with being special and favored. Even though I recognize these same tendencies in myself, I also feel my embarrassment to admit them. So how do I write honestly about the teeter-totter without turning off the very people who would most benefit from seeing themselves in the description? I think we gain courage to face our shame and pride when we see that we have not just been spoiled but that we also have been used. Our gifts and traits may have become a source of pride for someone whose good opinion we needed, while our corresponding weaknesses and needs were criticized or a source of shame. Our grandiosity and self-centeredness are not evil; rather, they are the way we learned to assume our place in a precarious world. They are learned responses to being overly valued for being cute, smart, funny, affectionate, talented, strong, or obedient, while we got little help with our less-comely attributes.

The story of the emperor's new clothes comes to mind here. We remember that two swindlers tell the emperor they have a very special and expensive cloth of unusual beauty, but it cannot be seen by people who are stupid or unfit for their position. Of course, neither the emperor nor anyone else wants to admit to stupidity or inadequacy, so everyone pretends to be dazzled by the emperor's new clothes until a child innocently remarks, "But he has nothing on!" It is easy to blame the emperor for vanity until we remember that everyone in the village also fears admitting they cannot see the special cloth. The emperor and all the people may be working hard to hide their feared stupidity, but the real culprits here are the swindlers who weave the tale that stupidity or poor performance are too shameful to be admitted and that specialness can be bought and sold. Most of us are villagers in this story, some of us are emperors, and a few of us are the child with the courage (or naiveté) to refute the idea that our inadequacies should be denied and hidden and that admiration for our specialness can be bartered for.

Perhaps the real culprit here is a culture that teaches, in the words of Korihor the Anti-Christ, "there could be no atonement made for the sins of men, but every man fared in this life according to the management of the creature; therefore every man prospered according to his genius, and that every man conquered according to his strength" (Alma 30:17).

As we learn to tolerate inadequacy and failure as normal and surmountable through effort, humor, learning, and help—rather than abnormal and to be hidden, lambasted, or denied—we begin to imagine that the teeter-totter is not the only toy on the playground. We can begin to imagine finding self-worth in building with others in the sand, pushing the limits of the swing, or making a fort in the trees. And when we fall or fail, the Atonement is not just a backup plan for the subhuman but the living, sacramental bread and water every single person needs to survive. In contrast with Korihor's claims, God does not define us or value us based only on our genius, strength, prosperity, and conquests. Christ has atoned for our weakness as well as for our sins.

In order to get to genuine self-forgiveness or self-acceptance, we must first qualify for God's forgiveness or acceptance, which we do by repentance and humility. We don't repent of or learn from our mistakes until we admit we are wrong—which is hard to do on the teeter-totter of pride and shame. Admitting we are wrong gets easier when we distinguish sin from weakness, allow success and failure to coexist in the same person, and increase our empathy for those we hurt. Let's review these three principles that help us productively admit mistakes.

PRINCIPLE #1: DISTINGUISHING SIN FROM WEAKNESS

Admission of error gets easier when we learn to distinguish sin from weakness. When I have only one big, amorphous category called "sin," hopelessness sets in as soon as I admit error or inadequacy. Distinguishing sin, for which I can completely repent, from weakness, which I may strengthen with God's help but may never eliminate, fosters hope. If I lump them both together, then everything looks like sin and everything I do wrong makes me a sinner. I cannot imagine how I can possibly repent of it all, so I just pretend I am above reproach (Delusion) or sink into shame (Despair).

If I recognize the category of "weakness," I make room for gradual improvement, acknowledgment of mistakes, the expectation of imperfection, and the merit of building on strengths. I don't have to apply scriptural passages about sin to my every flaw, mistake, or clumsiness. I begin to imagine God as patient and understanding, not just angry and disgusted. In short, I can be wrong without being bad, making it easier to admit I'm wrong. That brings me to the second principle: acknowledging that good and bad can coexist in one person.

PRINCIPLE #2: RECOGNIZING THE COEXISTENCE OF GOOD AND BAD

A second help in admitting mistakes is the ability to see failure and success as coexisting in one person without either one being all-defining. We spend a lot of time trying to distinguish good and evil so we can stay away from evil and cherish good. It can seem counterintuitive to foster a worldview that allows good and bad to coexist in the same person without the bad tainting or undoing all the good. But when we think any drop of ink in our pure water of goodness will ruin the whole of who we are, it is hard to admit being inky. While a single serious sin compromises our virtue, we can have weaknesses galore and still have strengths and gifts as well. Better to see ourselves as a mixed bag of multicolored stones—mistakes and successes, weakness and gifts, challenges and triumphs—than as a glass of inky water because of any mistake.

It is hard to see corrections as helpful instead of degrading and demoralizing unless we can deeply accept both strength and weakness, success and failure, trials and joys as part of the normal range of human experience for us and every person. To forgive ourselves for being less than average we must first accept ourselves for being average, and the average person is neither the embodiment of evil nor the personification of virtue. When even being *average* is an embarrassment, actual sins are simply too shameful to admit or repent of, and without repentance we can never get to self-forgiveness.

We can practice specific skills to increase our tolerance for being a mixed bag of strengths and weaknesses. First, we can practice acting nondefensively when corrected, even if at first we feel stung and angry. My husband is an expert at two simple phrases that come in handy here: "That's helpful. Let me think about that" and "Thank you for telling me that—tell me more." At first these phrases may give lip service only to humility, but they create a dignified space for us to retreat into and ponder. They give us time to comfort the part of us that hates being wrong, remember that we really do want to know how we can improve, and like and respect ourselves for getting better at humility.

The temple is a good place to practice nondefensiveness and the joys of being ordinary. In God's house, there are many rules in place to help things runs smoothly, and there are hundreds of workers and patrons and staff members going about with differing sensibilities about what is appropriate or what makes for a good experience. Sometimes we may run up against a rule or a person at odds with our own expectations. After all, we each have different ideas about what we need to feel welcome rather than criticized, and we all seem to believe that in the temple we have the right only to the former and never the latter. Yet God is also trying to teach us principles that may not come naturally to us—such as humility, repentance, reverence, order, modesty, charity, growth, and faith. In other words, in the temple there are countless opportunities to practice being wrong or inept without believing that also makes us bad. There are wonderful opportunities to learn about the joys of both not being in charge and not being passive, not drawing attention to ourselves and seeing the worth of every soul, not knowing everything and not being ashamed of it, not being perfect and still being blameless.

In my efforts to practice not being ashamed of being a mixed bag, I have had to take some coaching in what exactly being average means. If a bowler plays ten games, her average will be figured by adding up her scores and dividing by ten. Both the high games and the low games have to be counted. She is not just her best games, nor is she just her worst ones. Roughly figured, her scores for half of the games will be below her average and her scores for the other half will be above her average. In bowling, there is no way a player can always or even nearly always have an above-average game. *By definition, half of what she does will be below her personal average.*

This is a valuable lesson for people on the teeter-totter who are inclined to believe that every below-average performance is a preventable tragedy for which we deserve self-pity or self-castigation. We may be able to raise our personal average over time as we learn and practice, but by definition half of everything we do will be below our average. When we give a performance, teach a lesson, play a game, or do a report that is below average for us, it is not a sign that something awful has happened for which we need to feel ashamed. It doesn't mean we should give up as failures. It doesn't mean life owes us better. It is just a sign that the laws of mathematics are still holding. Good news.

As we begin to see more clearly our own excessive shame, we can feel ashamed of even that. This is one more opportunity to practice real humility and real confidence in the Lord. Even our shame is something we do not need to be ashamed of. It does not make us unsalvageable subhumans but is part and parcel of the mortal experience. It is normal to feel embarrassment and shame, and nobody really likes being wrong. This too we can approach with compassion for ourselves and gratitude for the Lord's patient tutoring.

Doing things we are not great at gives us the chance to enjoy playing the game independent of whether we win or lose. People on the teeter-totter don't get much experience with playing because for us life is a far too serious business. We need practice not keeping score and delighting instead in the pleasure of the moment.

PRINCIPLE #3: EMPATHY FOR
THOSE WE HURT

The third support in admitting sin or error so we can move out of Delusion is feeling real empathy for others—the kind of empathy that motivates us to repent when we hurt other people instead of seeing only how they are hurting us. Whereas compassion and empathy for those we hurt is a major motivator in repentance, seeing other people as competitors, embarrassments, or simply irrelevant to our self-worth agenda blocks our awareness of the need to change. We may feel great compassion for people who have been hurt by life but have little understanding of those who have been hurt by us. We are so aware of how others have embarrassed, misunderstood, or infuriated us that we can't take a step back to see ourselves through their eyes.

Sometimes we are so concerned about others' opinions or getting our own esteem needs met that we don't even stop to realize that others need us too. We have to make a conscientious effort to show interest in others, ask them questions, or extend ourselves to befriend them. We have to push ourselves to take on the less showy parts of a team project, or let others get a turn in the sun. But as we tune in to others as fellow humans and not just as pawns in our self-esteem project, we can find satisfaction in building others, not just in being built. We can begin to move past our vague unease with ourselves for not being as caring or connected as we know we should be and instead feel good about ourselves for doing something about our self-centeredness.

Envy of others is a natural result of life on the teeter-totter, where someone else's teeter always means our totter. In contrast, the gospel makes it clear that each of us has gifts and a mission to fulfill, and each of us has weaknesses to keep us humble. I have come to see envy as a bright signal that I need to get back to the rigors of my own mission, which I am probably avoiding or sidestepping. Envy also suggests that I am choosing to ignore the ways others have had to pay for what they have. When I am enviously focused on other people's accomplishments, prosperity, children, or beauty, seeing these as sure signs of God's unfair favoritism or my inherent worthlessness, I am usually choosing to ignore the prices such people have paid for what they have or the work they have invested. I may also be ignoring the weaknesses that go with their strengths or the heartaches they have had elsewhere. I just want to believe that they are lucky and I am not—something I can't help—and that this accounts for the differences between us.

AT ONE, NOT A-ONE

Christ is the *only* Only Begotten Son, the only perfect being. He knows that for some of us it is humiliating and difficult not to be perfect, and He doesn't hold His perfection or our imperfection against us. He wants us to find connection through what we have in common with the human race, not superiority in being separate from it, and He models this for us in the atonement He wrought. During that supreme act of joining us, He took upon Himself the pains, afflictions, sins, temptations, sicknesses, infirmities, and mortality of us all, that He might know how to succor us with true, in-the-flesh understanding of the human condition (Alma 6:11–13). Christ was sinless, but he was not weakness-less. He was tempted, sick, tired, limited, emotional, hungry, frustrated, afflicted. He was subject to what it means to be human. In other words, He does not ask us to endure any human indignity that He did not stoop to, either through the experience of life or the experience of the Atonement. He does not gain His exaltation, His place at the pinnacle of the teeter-totter, at our expense. In fact He doesn't really get on the teeter-totter after all. He comes over and sits on the ground with us, in all things.

We can submit to the ignominy of being human as we deepen our trust that the Only Begotten is not the Only Beloved. Christ did His job so we could do ours. In turn, He offers us all that the Father has as joint-heirs with Him. As we acknowledge our errors without catastrophizing, we accept that we don't need to be superior in everything to be loved, redeemed, or exalted. We get to experience the ordinary pleasure of not having to hide our weaknesses in order to be valued. We can learn to rejoice in our gifts while accepting our weaknesses as part of the package. We can afford to fail, so we can afford to try. And when we fail, as we all will, we can afford to admit it, repent of our sin and accept our weakness, gain forgiveness or grace from God, and forgive ourselves.

NEW ENDINGS

When I have a troubling dream, it is interesting to think about how I would rewrite the ending. This allows me to explore what needed to happen in the dream to resolve the problem at hand or finish the story in a new way. In the case of the emperor's new clothes, the story ends with the emperor continuing the parade back to his palace while he wonders disconcertedly if the child who announced his nakedness might have been right. When confronted with our nakedness we could also choose to hold our head high and finish the parade stark naked. We could instead blame our subjects for their stupidity and banish them. Or perhaps we might slink off to another kingdom where our own stupidity has not yet been exposed. When we live on the teeter-totter of shame and pride, these are the only endings to the story that we can really imagine.

So let's consider another ending: How about we all have a good laugh, kick out the swindlers, eat hot dogs and potato salad, and go jump in the pool? And vow that we will not get suckered again into advancing our self-esteem by making others' stupidity manifest.

Teeter-totters are fun on playgrounds, but they don't sit well in our souls.

SUMMARY

What are you most proud of in your life?

What are you most ashamed of?

What connections do you see between those first two answers?

How might you get better at admitting errors without undue shame?

7

DEPRESSION

*My life cannot implement in action the demands of all
the people to whom my heart responds.*

—ANNE MORROW LINDBERGH[1]

The sentence above by Anne Morrow Lindbergh can be read two ways—as a simple declaration of fact or as a resentful complaint, tinged with self-recrimination. When I am in a calm and truthful place I feel it as the former—a reminder that since there is no way for one mortal to address the needs of all those to whom compassion is due, I should help where I can but I cannot do it all.

I can also feel this statement much differently—as an exhausted, self-defensive surrender, tinged with the bitterness of despair. In Despair we can't see the point of trying to change because we don't think we can, yet we feel guilty and oppressed by our failings. Even depression with a strong biological component can be aggravated by thoughts of helplessness and hopelessness. Dismantling such thoughts can help us move out of Despair and toward the more peaceful quadrant of Self-Forgiveness and Self-Acceptance. Yet changing such thoughts is not quite as simple as just telling ourselves to quit being so negative. A whole field of psychology called cognitive behavioral therapy developed around trying to help people rewrite the thinking that underwrites depression.[2]

For those of us who tend to get depressed about being depressed, it helps to remember just how common depression is. Experts estimate that 10 to 25 percent of women and about half that many men will become clinically depressed at some point. At this moment, 5 to 10 percent of women and 2 to 3 percent of men meet the criteria for a major depressive disorder (the most common form of depression). Symptoms of clinical depression may include feelings of sadness, excessive guilt, loss of appetite, lack of energy, or irritability that last longer than two weeks, interfere with work or relationships. Other symptoms of clinical depression include difficulty making decisions, loss of pleasure or interest in activities one used to enjoy, trouble sleeping or sleeping too much, or thoughts of suicide. Feelings of helplessness, hopelessness, and worthlessness are hallmarks of depressive thinking, along with feelings of exhaustion, depletion, and inadequacy. Life can feel meaningless when we struggle with depression. Further, the excessive guilt and negative self-evaluations manifest in depression work against self-forgiveness and self-acceptance.

DEPRESSION VERSUS DISCOURAGEMENT

Occasional bouts of depressive thoughts and feelings do not constitute depression as defined by psychologists and physicians but are part of the mortal experience for virtually everyone. People who would not be considered clinically depressed may still dip into the discouragement level of the quadrant of Despair and at such times may benefit from the tools that help the depressed move toward

Self-Forgiveness and Self-Acceptance. This chapter is directed to those who periodically struggle with discouragement or self-doubt, whether or not they become clinically depressed. For example, the great prophet Nephi describes feelings some would associate with discouragement (although this is only one of several ways people might understand his outpouring of feelings) in the following verses:

> O wretched man that I am! Yea, my heart sorroweth because of my flesh; my soul grieveth because of mine iniquities.
>
> I am encompassed about, because of the temptations and the sins which do so easily beset me.
>
> And when I desire to rejoice, my heart groaneth because of my sins. . . .
>
> . . . Why should my heart weep and my soul linger in the valley of sorrow, and my flesh waste away, and my strength slacken, because of mine afflictions?
>
> And why should I yield to sin because of my flesh? Yea, why should I give way to temptations, that the evil one have place in my heart to destroy my peace and afflict my soul? Why am I angry because of mine enemy? (2 Nephi 4:17–19, 26–27).

While we don't know exactly what prompted these feelings for Nephi, most of us can relate at times to his expressions of sadness, guilt, heaviness, sorrow, preoccupation with failures or sins, tearfulness, lack of energy, and irritability. Accordingly, we can also benefit from considering excerpts of Nephi's powerful testimony and prayer as an antidote to such thoughts and feelings:

> Nevertheless, I know in whom I have trusted.
>
> My God hath been my support; he hath led me through mine afflictions. . . .

He hath filled me with his love. . . .

Awake, my soul! No longer droop in sin. Rejoice, O my heart, and give place no more for the enemy of my soul. . . .

Rejoice, O my heart, and cry unto the Lord, and say: O Lord, I will praise thee forever; yea, my soul will rejoice in thee, my God, and the rock of my salvation.

May the gates of hell be shut continually before me, because that my heart is broken and my spirit is contrite! (2 Nephi 4:19–21, 28, 30, 32).

Nephi's trust in God's support, love, and salvation, along with his own humility and contrition, serve as an example of the kind of thoughts that can help all of us, whether depressed or merely discouraged, to combat the evil one and renew our hope. This chapter will focus on promoting such thoughts and positive self-talk to help us combat discouragement, stay out of depression, and avoid the excessive guilt that promotes hopelessness and helplessness rather than the repentance and faith in Christ Nephi models.

DEPRESSION AND GUILT

While people have reason to feel guilty when they have violated their moral code, guilty *feelings* do not always reliably reflect the actual state of our soul. When guilty feelings are consistently out of proportion to actual wrongdoing and are part of a larger pattern of persistent sadness, hopelessness, and helplessness, guilt may be a symptom of clinical depression. The depressed often feel unwarranted self-reproach over letting others down, get preoccupied with past errors, and tend to see current problems as punishment. When we are discouraged or temporarily down we too can think our weaknesses are really sins, and that neither is reparable. Whether or not it is of clinical proportions, depression is depressing![3]

While the light of Christ is the basis of conscience, conscience is also shaped by experience, learning, and social norms that may or may not be consistent with the gospel of Christ. Mark Twain's fictional character Huckleberry Finn is often quoted as having learned that "you can't pray a lie" when he tries to pray for forgiveness without really intending to change his sinful ways.[5] Yet in the story the "sin" Huck won't relinquish is helping his black friend Jim escape slavery. As Huck remembers Jim's true friendship and goodness, he decides that he won't turn Jim in—even if it means, as he has been taught, that he will go to hell for it. This is hardly something we would think of feeling guilty about today! In fact, we are glad about Huck's decision, which we see as morally superior to its alternative. Huck's conscience, shaped by the social norms of his day, is not necessarily an accurate guide to moral behavior or the appropriateness of guilty feelings.

Many depressive people have what psychologists call an "overly punitive superego," or a conscience that is excessively harsh and self-castigating. They feel unreasonable guilt and shame over trivial events and can be overwhelmed by the impossibility of implementing into action the needs of all the people to whom their hearts respond. Scriptures about the sin of hypocrisy convict them for not conforming perfectly to every belief they espouse. Satisfaction in the service they render or a job well done equates to reprehensible pride. Passing on a service sign-up sheet indelibly stamps them as selfish. And a modern equivalent of the dilemma Huck Finn faced would stop them in their tracks. Whether opting for honesty (turning Jim in) or compassion (helping him escape), they feel guilty for what they *didn't* do.

Theories about the causes and treatments of depression differ about whether irrational guilt causes depression or results from it. Excessive guilt can be a warning sign that depression is on the loose, even if it has not yet taken us hostage. Realistic management of guilty feelings gives people prone to depression a vital tool in avoiding it. Even if we don't max out at clinical depression, guilt that is irrational and excessive gets in our way, boxing us in at Despair rather than paving the way toward true repentance.

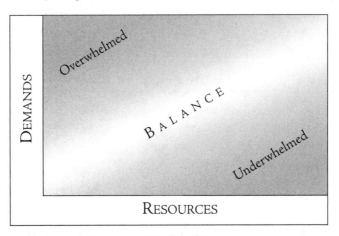

Diagram 4: Model of Depression

In researching adolescent depression, I used a simple model to express some aspects of the depressive dilemma.[4] This demands-resources model suggests that when we perceive that our demands and resources are in approximate balance we usually feel pretty good. Life is enjoyable and energizing when we have the skills, emotional reserves, social support, creativity, health, time, money, earning power, intelligence, spiritual beliefs, and other resources to manage such demands as the expectations of self, spouse, children, parents, bosses, friends, Church leaders, landlords, neighbors, and the IRS. When we apply our strengths to reasonable challenges, life is often characterized by the positive sense of flow associated with losing ourselves in work we enjoy.[6]

When it feels like we do not have adequate resources to meet our demands (Overwhelmed), or, in contrast, when we are not pushing ourselves to use and develop our wisdom and skills (Under-whelmed), depression often ensues. In the Overwhelmed quadrant we feel exhausted and depleted, inadequate to our tasks. We are heading toward the big three of depression: hopelessness, helpless-ness, and worthlessness. In the Underwhelmed quadrant we have feelings of meaninglessness and boredom associated with not being stretched, needed, or connected in caring relationships.

In all of this, our perception about our demands and resources is what counts. We may have more than adequate resources to meet our demands, but if we don't *think* we do, then we may still feel over-whelmed and become hopeless and despairing. Or we may *think* we have a lot of skills and wisdom to share, but if we aren't invest-ing them in things we care about we can end up feeling disconnected, devalued, and depressed.

REBALANCING

The model suggests three levers for change when we feel depressed. If we imagine demands and resources weighed against each other in an old-fashioned balancing scale, then we can shift the balance by either (1) adding or subtracting the *demands* that anchor one side of the scale; (2) changing the number or kind of *resources* on the other side of the scale; or (3) shifting the fulcrum that bal-ances demands and resources—which might be analogous to alter-ing our perceptions or our *attitude*. Making such changes rather than wallowing in self-pity about our awfulness helps us out of depres-sion and the quadrant of Despair and into positive action. Realistic goals, along with personal beliefs and life structures to accomplish them, help counteract the hopelessness and self-devaluing of depression.

Which of your demands do you experience as excessive,

onerous, or out of your comfort zone? Could you *reduce* any of these demands to make life more palatable? How might you *increase your resources* for meeting that demand by gaining skills, reading books, getting emotional support, and so forth? Could you *change your attitude* by focusing on gratitude, seeing demands as challenges instead of obstacles, shifting to a long-term view, looking for what is funny, seeing what you are learning instead of what you are losing, and so forth? If you are in the Underwhelmed position, how can you increase demands and find work to do that is more of a challenge, even though it means putting up with some anxiety, taking some risks, and being inconvenienced?

What does this have to do with self-forgiveness? When demands and resources are out of balance, depressive individuals have a tendency to blame themselves. As they shift demands, increase resources, or recalibrate attitudes to get life into a better balance, they feel less exhausted (if overwhelmed), or more useful (if underwhelmed). There are simply fewer reasons to feel bad about oneself when energy and skill are reasonably matched to the tasks and demands at hand. The fear of not measuring up and disappointing self and others declines. Finding legitimate uses for one's talents and love allows growth and a sense of contribution that give life meaning. Guilt over having more than one's share of the world's resources declines.

OPPOSING NEEDS

Human beings seem to have two opposing needs. One is to create. It encourages procreation and work and pulls us toward the risk, tension, ambiguity, and effort of growth. The other need is to rest, which includes our desires for stillness, peace, and a return to a tensionless state. We live in a tenuous balance between creating and resting, anxiety and peace, tension and release.

Depression can be seen as the triumph of the pull to rest over the pull to create, a desire for stillness and freedom from tension that becomes so dominant we want to give up, not feel, and stop trying to make sense of our lives.

We sense the balance and flow between creating and resting, energy and stillness, in our opposing needs to both acquire and simplify, our complementary needs for both confidence and humility. The wish for stillness and rest is utterly legitimate, but it can also backfire in two ways—either because we need rest and won't let ourselves stop all the striving without self-blame, or because we sink into stillness and then can't get moving again. Sometimes these problems alternate in the depressed individual who won't move precisely because of fear that once in motion there will be no permission to rest again. Doing so much that we wear ourselves out is a recipe for depression. Lack of goals, structure, plans, and routines is too. Both choices are supported by faulty beliefs that our worth is attached to our output, or unrealistic expectations about how much we can do.

Connie struggled with a deep and unremitting depression that virtually immobilized her for years. She spent most of her time reading in bed, her kindly husband doing what he could to make ends meet and keep up with household tasks. Connie felt guilty leaving her husband to do so much, but she also felt irritated and critical of him and then more guilty than ever. Caught in this vicious circle, she felt useless and hopeless and that life had little meaning. She also felt overwhelmed with self-expectations she could never live up to. When a new medication helped lift Connie's depression some, she began to notice the load her husband carried and to feel some genuine sympathy for him. Connie decided that even if she couldn't carry her full weight in the marriage, perhaps she could do something. After all, any effort she made would be better than lying in bed.

Not being domestically inclined, she felt that it would be easier to get a part-time job for which she had adequate skills than to help around the house. To her surprise, Connie was able to find employment. She had such low expectations that it was relatively easy not to disappoint herself as in previous years. Some days she still called in sick, but she also received many compliments for her conscientious work. As she got more secure in her ability she moved up to a new job with a boss who truly valued Connie's considerable intelligence and skill. The goals and structured routines of work coupled with this support and encouragement helped Connie keep her self-critical nature in check. Though it has been a long road, Connie has leveraged small goals, the basic routines of a job, and a simple desire to help into an extremely successful, meaningful life.

When I asked Connie how she managed to turn her life around after so many years of depression, she said a big piece was to stop looking for what was wrong with her. Even asking that question just demoralized her and put her on the defensive. Instead she gave herself permission to follow the smallest thread of compassion for her husband and to begin by doing the smallest things she could imagine to try to help out. She shut out the voices telling her such small efforts didn't count, and she told herself instead that anything was better than nothing. Setting small goals, maintaining simple routines, and reducing some self-demands while increasing others helped Connie find a new balance for her life where depression and guilt are not running the whole show.

BY SMALL AND SIMPLE MEANS

A colleague once decided to offer a class to his ward members on reducing guilt. He prepared a curriculum and some handouts and hoped a few people would show up. Half the ward came. When he offered a similar class for his colleagues at a professional conference, he met a standing-room-only crowd. He was not an exceptionally charismatic teacher—he just stumbled on a topic that touched a nerve for many people. To make sure his program was successful at delivering what it promised—reduced guilt—he asked people to score themselves on guilt and depression at the beginning and end of his class. Virtually everyone experienced substantially reduced guilt and depression.

What was his secret? He asked class members on the first day to identify some things they felt guilty about, and then he helped them design a simple program to spend fifteen minutes to start working on those things. That's it. Those who felt guilty about not doing their family history made concrete plans to take fifteen minutes that week to dig out their old family group sheets. Those who felt guilty about not having family home evening took fifteen minutes to gather their children for prayer and singing. Those who felt guilty about boatloads of stuff made the list, prioritized it, and then spent fifteen minutes working on the first item. People who felt guilty about less concrete things (like getting angry or overeating) spent fifteen minutes just learning more about their problem. One sister with a serious pornography addiction came up to him afterward to ask for help, and she set a goal the first week of simply waiting fifteen minutes after she was tempted before giving in. She did not conquer her addiction that week, but it was the first time in years that she had made any inroads at seeing herself as having some choice in her behavior.

No one finished off their list or repented of all their sins, but everyone spent a few minutes doing *something* instead of just feeling guilty and doing nothing. The class was a huge hit, and a group of demoralized Saints who had resigned themselves to a life of guilt learned that small steps in the right direction can turn nonproductive guilt into energizing change. We don't have to finish the repentance process before we can enjoy the blessings of hope and humility that come from being willing to do just a little, instead of thinking we have to do it all. Tackling our weakness a little at a time is a good way to combat the all-or-nothing thinking that leads to depression.

THOUGHTS UNDERLYING DEPRESSION

All-or-nothing thinking is common in people with depression. After all, if I believe I'm a sinner who does nothing to repent, then it is only reasonable that I not approve of myself and feel bad. Such thoughts lead logically to depressed feelings. Psychologists have learned that feelings of sadness, guilt, and despair follow naturally from believing ourselves when we think we are evil, selfish, worthless, incompetent, sinful, or unable to change. After all, if those things really do define us, then wouldn't any decent, moral person feel awful?

The snag is that we don't even notice that we are thinking this way, and so we don't stop to see if our thinking makes sense given the whole of who we are. We don't examine the evidence pro and con, get opinions from others, check out what's possible, or experiment to see if we're right or wrong. We just swallow our negative self-assessment hook, line, and sinker, and then haul ourselves flopping and flailing into the deadly bucket of Despair. Some of the common cognitive distortions, or automatic but unexamined beliefs of the depressed, include:

- All-or-nothing thinking ("Now I've ruined everything.")
- Labeling ("I'm such a failure.")
- Mind reading ("They must think I'm so selfish.")

+ Helplessness ("I can't control my temper.")
+ Hopelessness ("My life will never get better.")
+ Fortune-telling ("Now I'll lose my job for sure.")

We may see these statements as exaggerations when they are on paper but not when they are floating around unexamined in our heads. A good cognitive therapy workbook (see endnotes for this chapter), a good therapist, or even a good friend may be able to help us uncover the distortions in our thinking by objectively asking such things as:

+ What is the evidence that this is true? What is the evidence it is not true?
+ What do you tell yourself this situation means about you? Is there another possibility?
+ When did you learn to see the world this way? What about this situation is different from that one?

As we jot down our thoughts, examine the evidence pro and con, and rewrite our thoughts to more accurately reflect a broader slice of reality, we end up with statements that look more like this:

+ I messed up this time, but usually I do okay.
+ I fail at some things and succeed at others, like everyone does.
+ I wonder what they think of me. Maybe I'll ask.
+ If I break this down into smaller pieces, maybe I can do it.
+ Most things work themselves out over time.
+ If I apologize and improve I can probably keep my job.

This process is simple, but it is not easy. Even after years of using cognitive behavioral therapy techniques with clients and myself, I frequently catch myself believing distorted and unexamined thoughts for which the evidence is mixed at best. Even worse is when I don't catch these thoughts—I just get trapped in the feelings that flow from them without ever seeing the connection between my current feeling and my recent thinking.

I offer a warning to well-meaning helpers, however: just telling someone in the throes of unexamined, irrational thoughts what *you* think usually won't help. We risk accusations of being Pollyannas who don't understand how bad things are. Instead, help them

+ realize what they believe in a given situation says about them;
+ examine the evidence for the truthfulness or falsity of those thoughts;
+ figure out how they learned to see the world that way and how their current circumstance is different;
+ rewrite their thoughts to more accurate ones.

RECEIVING GOD'S LOVE

Depression interferes with our acceptance of God's grace when that depression is accompanied by the deep belief that we can never be good enough to earn it. Depression often precludes the important recognition that none of us deserves God's grace, but it is freely given to all the humble who acknowledge their weakness and come to Him for help. We all need that help, all of the time.

Sadness, guilt, even deep self-rejection are appropriate when we sin and should help us to be motivated to repent. Unfortunately, depressive thinking also tends to turn every weakness into a sin, demoralizing us with the belief that we must be truly evil to have so much wrong with us. Although none of us can eliminate all our weaknesses, Christ's atonement applies to both sin (when we repent) and weakness (when we are humble and teachable). God does not just offer the gifts of loving forgiveness and grace to a special few, chosen on the basis of some special status or lineage. He offers them to all who make sincere efforts to follow Him.

Elder Marion D. Hanks once told the story in general conference of an interaction with two of his young daughters, a story he said gave him "a tendency to tears." It is a story that may apply to many with a tendency to depression who believe that God's promises somehow do not apply to them because they can never be good enough to deserve them. Elder Hanks recalls:

> Another little girl had joined our family and was of course much loved. Occasionally I had called her older sister "Princess," but had thought about that, and, since the second young lady was equally deserving of royal treatment, had concluded that it would be well for her to share the title, if it were used at all.
>
> So one day I called to her, "Come on, Princess. Let's go to the store for mother." She seemed not to hear. "Honey," her mother said, "daddy is calling you."
>
> "Oh," she answered, with a quiet sadness that hurt my heart, "he doesn't mean me."
>
> In memory I can still see the resignation on her innocent child face and hear it in her voice, when she thought that her father didn't mean her.
>
> . . . My child at first did not understand that my invitation was meant for her. She thought it was for someone else. "He didn't mean me." If any within the sound of my voice today need assurance that God's call to repentance and his invitation to mercy and forgiveness and love is for them, I bear you that solemn witness, in the name of Jesus Christ.[7]

Alma teaches that "by small and simple things are great things brought to pass; and small means in many instances doth confound the wise" (Alma 37:6). The patterns of depression and irrational guilt do not lend themselves to easy fixes, but often a small change in our understanding of ourselves, God, and our relationships with others produces a big change in our prospects for the future. Self-reflection, prayer, reading, listening, therapy, and trying new approaches can help us see our blind spots, accept and heal old feelings, change our self-images and images of God, and relate differently. Small acts of repentance and humble, personal growth can hold big keys to meeting more of the needs of "all the people to whom [our] heart responds."[8] And small choices to trust God's love for us despite our sins and weaknesses help us realize that God's heart responds to us as well.

SUMMARY

What is a sin or weakness of omission or commission that nags you with feelings of guilt?

What could you do this week in fifteen minutes to get started on repentance or change?

What do you tell yourself this sin or weakness means about you?

Is there any evidence that this conclusion might not be completely accurate? What is the evidence?

How might you encourage yourself to envision that God's love and promise of grace and forgiveness apply to you personally?

8

ANXIOUS PERFECTIONISM

He hath not dealt with us after our sins;
nor rewarded us according to our iniquities.
For as the heaven is high above the earth,
so great is his mercy toward them that fear him.
As far as the east is from the west,
so far hath he removed our transgressions from us.
Like as a father pitieth his children,
so the Lord pitieth them that fear him.
For he knoweth our frame;
he remembereth that we are dust.

—Psalm 103:10–14

I live in a beautiful neighborhood with tall pine trees and beautiful mountain vistas, so morning walks are a highlight of my day. Once home I often stop to pull a few weeds, giving me at least the illusion of doing something constructive for my yard each morning. After pulling as many weeds as I can hold in one hand, I take them to the garbage can by my back door and call it quits.

We are new to our area, and I was not familiar with a certain weed growing in the yard until my walking partner pointed it out. This weed is the morning glory. Some people cultivate morning glories for their flowers, but in my neighborhood they are a pervasive and persistent pest that entwines around other plants, choking them and stripping their leaves. Once I learned to recognize morning glories I started seeing them everywhere. My morning handful of weeds got bigger and bigger as I battled the morning glories each morning before heading inside.

One morning I had already taken the garbage can to the curb when I began weeding. That meant that after taking my weeds to the garbage can, I had to walk through the yard again on my way to the house. My eye, now well trained, caught glimpses of more morning glories in hiding. I started on a second armload of weeds. But on returning from the garbage can again, I saw there were still more morning glories to be found. I kept pulling, my back now starting to get tired. But each time I headed back to the house after my trip to the garbage can, more weeds ambushed me. I couldn't ignore them. I kept pulling.

OBSESSIVE-COMPULSIVE DISORDERS AND EXCESSIVE GUILT

I learned a little something that morning about what it might feel like to have an obsessive-compulsive disorder (OCD)—to have an idea or an impulse that keeps circling around in one's mind and cannot be ignored but that increasingly affects one's agency, behavior, and thoughts. Soon, all one can see are the morning glories, ever-present possibilities of something dangerous lurking in the shadows that must be tackled and rooted out but that never goes away.

The symptoms of obsessive-compulsive disorders are probably familiar. People with such disorders may become preoccupied with counting or checking, never fully comfortable that dangers have been contained. They may wash their hands so often in an effort to control germs that their skin becomes raw. They may be flooded with thoughts or images of hurting someone or with vulgar language or sexual images, and the more they try to control these thoughts (which horrify them and are completely foreign to their values), the more the thoughts predominate, convincing them that they are evil to have such preoccupations. Some can't throw anything away lest some day they might need it, while others are simply preoccupied with work, rules, orderliness, or productivity to the exclusion of leisure, pleasure, or spontaneity.

Like many human characteristics, obsessive-compulsive disorders are an extreme of a normal human experience that in its quieter manifestations has a positive value. We *want* our brains to remind us to check the stove, wash our hands, not swear, store things for future use, or persist with a difficult task and see it through to the end. We *value* high moral standards, a solid work ethic, and excellence. But at the high end of the scale of normal checking, cleaning, persisting, and obeying is an extreme that becomes very painful and unmanageable for some.

Though relatively few of us have an obsessive-compulsive *disorder*, more of us have obsessive-compulsive or perfectionist *tendencies* that can lead to excessive guilt or worry and interfere with our peace. Among other things, compulsive perfectionism can include difficulty knowing when to quit, excessively high self-expectations, irrational guilt, or preoccupation with one's weaknesses. While the exacting standards of some perfectionists lead to high achievement and great accomplishments, perfectionism can also make us overly critical of ourselves and others, taking over our lives with preoccupations of little importance. Like the morning glories, which are lovely flowers when properly cultivated and contained but a threat to the whole garden when out of control, perfectionism can so dominate one's life so as to almost preclude healthy growth and peace. The perfectionists I'm referring to here are not necessarily the ones who drive others crazy with their demands or criticisms, or who think of themselves as perfectionists. The people I'm referring to are more inclined to think of themselves as barely cutting it, in fact. They may be very tolerant with others' imperfections but have little tolerance for their own.

Some psychotherapists believe that overly perfectionist people use obsessive rituals to try to atone for "thought crimes" like selfishness or anger. It is hard for obsessive perfectionists to imagine that selfishness and anger are normal human emotions or that selfish or angry thoughts are substantially different from selfish or angry behavior. They work overtime to counteract or pay for such thoughts rather than accepting them as normal, keeping them in perspective, or finding appropriate ways to express them.

Medical science is increasingly convinced that obsessive-compulsive disorders are related to some malfunction in the brain, not just choices or character traits. Nevertheless, people with these disorders share common unrealistic beliefs and expectations that support their behavior, and these beliefs are subject to modification. For example, many perfectionist obsessives believe (without fully realizing it) in what one expert calls "The Myth of Control."[1] This myth includes two primary beliefs: (1) that it is possible to avoid all errors and harm, large and small, if one is careful enough and tries hard enough, and (2) that doing so will keep one safe from danger, criticism, and failure.

The Myth of Control is supposed to keep the anxiety of living in an unfair and uncontrollable world at bay. If something bad does happen (someone criticizes me, my spouse gets sick, I have an angry or selfish thought, or I don't get a promotion), I can keep the myth in place by finding something to blame myself for, giving me the illusion of control (this happened because I didn't wash my hands enough, check sufficiently, count correctly, study adequately, serve with true humility, pray with enough faith, and so forth). If I redouble my efforts, I can almost feel back in control. In this way, the world feels less unpredictable and frightening, even though the cost of this illusion of control is scathing self-blame and a relentless pressure to do everything perfectly. In this mind-set, errors or unhappy thoughts are not seen as survivable or something to learn from but as something to prevent at all costs. Errors or negative emotions feel intolerable, yet ever-threatening. The desperate effort to control things that we cannot completely control (thoughts, surroundings, other people, or the future) makes us feel more out of control than ever.

Even without a full-blown disorder, obsessive-compulsive tendencies make it difficult for people to know when enough is enough. Such tendencies get us hyperfocused on small details that are not really important or—especially pertinent to our subject—create excessive guilt and difficulty in putting self-condemning thoughts to rest. When we have truly repented but are still plagued with worry and guilt that focuses our attention on an endless minutia of self-expectations, or when we can't let go of images of our past or potential failures, we may be dealing with obsessive-compulsive tendencies. We get locked into the Distrust box, believing we can never be good enough to merit God's mercy. This is not healthy guilt—the kind that prods us to repent and improve—but an obsessive preoccupation we need to dismantle and ignore. As creativity expert Julia Cameron warns, "Perfectionism is not a quest for the best. It is a pursuit of the worst in ourselves, the part that tells us that nothing we do will ever be good enough."[2]

THE MYTH OF CONTROL AND GOD

Melissa wards off most of her worries about germs with an ever-present bottle of hand sanitizer. Warding off her worries about God's displeasure if she does not do enough is harder. There are not enough hours in the day for all she commits to do, but saying no to anything makes her anxious. She worries that God will be angry with her and not protect her children from predators or accidents unless she works overtime to show her devotion. Images of her children getting hurt flood her mind at times, driving her to work harder. When her son fell off his bike and broke his arm, she wondered if God wanted her to see that underneath her outward smiles she was really uncharitably, sinfully resentful about all her responsibilities. Her husband is frustrated because their home and marriage are sorely neglected, but Melissa doesn't stop until—despite the hand sanitizer—she gets sick.

Melissa's preoccupation with serving temporarily relieves her anxiety—if she works hard enough she can ward off potential dangers and get relief from what she fears is unconscionable selfishness for not always being thrilled and delighted about performing her duties to others. But her preoccupation also creates anxiety, precisely because there is too much to manage. She tries harder and harder to serve in order to buy godly favor or avert godly criticism, but she can be sufficiently dedicated in one domain only by neglecting others, leaving her open to self-criticism for the things she ignores. The toll of all this vigilance eventually catches up with her, leaving her exhausted and demoralized. She may make a temporary stab at not trying so hard or letting some things slide, only to hear a talk in church on the need for more compassionate service or the importance of not ignoring any commandment. Then she is off to the races again, afraid of the price she will pay for slacking off.

For a person with OCD tendencies, full-time missions can be a special challenge. Messages about the importance of 100 percent obedience and serving with no regrets are motivating to most missionaries who are somewhere on the normal scale between good-but-undisciplined desires and concerted-but-realistic enthusiasm. But people with strong OCD or perfectionist tendencies have difficulty moderating these messages with a realistic understanding that 100 percent obedience was possible only for Jesus Christ, and that regret is simply the price we all pay to learn and grow. Determined to live all the rules exactly, they lose sight of the principles that guide the rules. The joy of serving is swallowed up in exhaustion and despair. Correction from others becomes evidence of failure, not an opportunity to improve. Other people become enemies to hide from, not sources of mutual love and support. Faith in God's love is replaced by fear of God's anger and retaliation. Every stumble over a forgotten scripture becomes evidence that God is withholding His Spirit because of failure to work hard enough.

In this frame of mind, the missionary feels safer if he keeps himself "harrowed up" at all times so he will be less likely to err. He hopes to convince the heavens that he isn't as sinful as he feels and doesn't need further punishment. He cannot imagine accepting that he will make mistakes, feel angry or resentful at times, or even fail at something important—and that he can simply survive these events and feelings and learn from them. Such manifestations of normal human weakness feel to him like horrific sins. Nor can he imagine that a perfect God could accept nonchalance about errors. The pain and anxiety associated with making a mistake, drawing criticism from others, having a negative feeling, or risking offense to God feel intolerable—and avoidable if he is constantly on guard. He doesn't realize that one of his most important tasks is to increase his tolerance for mortal limits and weakness by enduring anxiety and learning from pain, increasing his skills for coping with criticism, gaining insight about feelings of anger or selfishness, and strengthening his confidence in God's love and atoning power—not just to increase his perfection and repent from sin.

COMBATING OBSESSIONS AND COMPULSIONS

A crucial way to combat perfectionist obsessions is to examine our view of God. One young woman who struggles with OCD realized that when she saw God as a finger-shaking judge, her OCD thoughts ran wild and she was filled with anxiety and self-doubt. All the messages she heard on a daily basis about keeping the commandments grew barbs for her and would not let her free. But when she could connect deeply with God's love, kindness, goodness, and delight in His children *and in her,* even with her God-given mortal weakness, the barbs retreated a bit and a scent of sweetness returned. She writes:

"I started thinking about an important concept in relation to God—that He's not looking to condemn us in everything we do. If the guilt we feel inspires us to move forward and strengthens our faith in God, then it is a good kind of guilt to motivate us to change. But if the guilt only brings us down and farther away from God, then something about this guilt isn't associated with God."

As she came to trust the God of love as her Father and Friend, He became her ally in her struggle with OCD instead of a five-star general in the enemy camp trying to prove her defectiveness.

Other techniques that help people combat the symptoms of OCD can also help those with moderate obsessive-compulsive tendencies to subdue chronic irrational guilt and live more peacefully. Let's consider some ABCs of dealing with excessive, obsessive guilt: *Allow, Balance, Correct, Distract,* and *Enjoy.* These can help us be more accepting of mortal weakness and more trusting of God's forgiveness and grace so we can move out of the box of Distrust and into the box of Self-forgiveness or Self-acceptance.

ALLOW

A first step in dealing with obsessive, perfectionist guilt is to simply *allow* the painful awareness of our mortal weakness or imperfection to register without fighting it or hating ourselves for it. Self-hatred is like a raging fever that becomes more life-threatening than the original infection that fever is supposed to fight. In a similar way, the self-harrowing we do to make sure we never err again can become more threatening to our spiritual and mental health than the initial error we committed. Increasing our tolerance for the pain of making a mistake keeps the hot fever of guilt from getting out of control.

Ironically, when we combat our guilty feelings with self-berating thoughts (designed to never let ourselves get in this predicament again), we undermine our hope and confidence in the Lord's love and set ourselves up to stop trying. When we simply allow ourselves to sit quietly with the pain of criticism or disappointment without self-hatred or resistance, we can avoid adding insult to injury and get a more truthful perspective on our situation. As we name our feeling (resentment, hurt, anger, fear) without either condemning or encouraging it, we learn that we can tolerate the pain of criticism or self-disappointment without overreacting, like learning to breathe through labor pain rather than trying to stop it. This is not to say that the pain is not real, only that it gets worse when we fear and resist it. Learning to breathe through our disappointment in ourselves or fear of other's criticism is a worthy goal.

A missionary who went home early because of severe OCD and

panic attacks was devastated when a relative told him that "families never get over the shame of having a missionary come home early." Certain that others felt the same way but were too polite to say it, he retreated into a private world of self-recrimination. Every family gathering renewed his painful feelings, and soon he had no desire to be around family at all. He moved to a distant state, hoping to avoid the pain of his relative's judgment, but he could not move away from his own memories. It took a long time to learn to simply feel the pain the relative's statement evoked in him without trying to fix it, escape it, or change it, but eventually he decided he didn't have to organize his whole life around making the pain and shock he felt from that comment go away. He could simply say, "That hurt, but I can tolerate hurt. And just because it hurt does not mean it is true. It is pretty normal that I would feel hurt by such a comment. I can tolerate this feeling. I came home from my mission because of a mortal limitation, not a sin."

BALANCE

If humility is the bedrock of learning, humiliation is the quick-sand into which our efforts at change collapse into despair. We see little point in working to improve when convinced we are worthless failures. As we *balance* awareness of our shortcomings with awareness of our strengths, we can turn our attention away from the sinking threat of failure and toward the building blocks of hope.

When stinging with some reminder of my weakness, making a list of ten things I do well or blessings I deeply appreciate gives me hope that success and failure are not all-or-nothing propositions. When guilt about my weakness or unhappy feelings threaten to swamp me, I remember that everyone is given both weaknesses and gifts and that all feelings can be instructive and appropriate at times. No one receives only gifts and loving feelings without weaknesses and hard feelings to deal with as well. President Howard W. Hunter was in a wheelchair, but he taught us all the importance of being worthy to walk into the house of the Lord. President Gordon B. Hinckley's small temples will never rival the grandeur of the Salt Lake Temple, but they will still bless millions of Saints, both living and dead. Even God's anger, which I fear so much at times, reminds me that my own anger can also be appropriate and worth examining. Contributing my strengths and my love matters more than eliminating all my weaknesses and hard feelings.

CORRECT

The need to *correct* our course is not a sign that we are lousy pilots. On its flight from New York to Paris, a plane is exactly on course only a tiny fraction of the time. Only because the pilot (or autopilot) has the ability to constantly correct the course does the plane arrive at its destination. Yet when we have a perfectionist, obsessive mind-set, having to correct our course can feel like having our pilot's license revoked for incompetence.

Another challenge for obsessives is thinking that every time we are off course we need to make the *same* correction: live the rule at hand more perfectly. This is roughly equivalent to a pilot always turning right whenever he realizes he is off course (which would eventually just take him back to where he started). Sometimes the course corrections we need are to turn left, slow down to conserve fuel, increase altitude to get above a storm, or detour to London to pick up passengers. Likewise, the course corrections we need may not always be to strive harder and with more strictness but rather to turn toward more flexibility, slow down on volunteering for a while, get perspective on a storm of hard feelings rather than trying to make them disappear, or make a detour from our goal to spend time with friends.

DISTRACT

Checking to see if the back door is locked before we leave our apartment is a good idea. Checking the door four times is a waste of time and energy. Checking the door ten times may keep us from ever getting to our destination. Guilt can be like checking the lock on a door. Guilty thoughts that encourage course corrections and that are relieved when we get back on track are helpful. Guilty thinking that stops us from progressing and grinds us to a halt should be treated as an obsession that we should try to ignore and *distract* ourselves from—not as a helpful reminder from our conscience, not a sure sign that we are irreparably bad, and not a noble token of our superior standards. Sometimes guilt is just an intrusive and tempting thought habit that we are better off ignoring.

People who struggle with obsessive thoughts of any kind (unwanted images, obscene language, self-destructive temptations, and so forth) must learn one thing: you can't stop thinking about a pink elephant by trying not to think about a pink elephant. Try it if you don't believe me. Try as hard as you want not to think about a pink elephant. Are you trying really, really hard not to think about that pink elephant? How is your not thinking about a pink elephant going? You get the picture.

The only way not to think about a pink elephant is to casually think about something else instead, gently drawing our attention to the birds outside the window, some fascinating problem at work, or the love we feel for a child. When guilt has become a futile obsession, distraction is the best course. Simply make a mental note that says "tempting guilty thought" whenever irrational guilt starts sloshing around. Receive the feeling instead of resisting it, label it as nonconstructive noise, and then gently, smilingly turn attention to other things. This approach is far more effective than horrified insistence that we *must* not think guilty thoughts.

ENJOY

When we think our job in life is to keep our car in mint condition and never put a scratch on it, we won't find much pleasure in dirt roads. Yet there are some destinations we cannot reach by staying on clean pavement. Elder Bruce C. Hafen writes:

"I . . . have little sympathy for [students with a 4.0 grade point average] who receive their first A-. I have seen them in tears at that blessed event. My reaction is to tell them, 'Well, your shiny new car has its first dent. Now you can get along with your journey like the rest of us, concentrating on the sights and sounds of your travels without worrying about your car getting dusty along the bumpy road. Welcome to real life.'"[3]

Reminding ourselves how wonderful it feels to improve rather than how awful it feels to fail can help us stay focused on growth and learning rather than on avoiding risks and pain. Making a list of lessons learned can help us reconnect with the blessings of the journey, even when our shiny new car picks up a few nicks or a tire blows. The purpose of the car is to get us to our destination of learning by experience and faith in Christ—not to keep the car as spotless as possible. No matter what happens to our car, we are always under warranty with God.

To take advantage of this warranty, however, we must abandon the Myth of Control and put our trust in God—not in our own relentless perfection—to keep us safe. This is a scary proposition because in fact God has never promised to keep us safe, but only to save us. Relying on the Myth of Control is relying on a lie. Even if we could keep our car shiny, doing so will not ward off all criticism, harm, hard feelings, or danger. Nor does being hurt, criticized, angry, or selfish automatically mean we have failed in our vigilance and need to try harder, do penance, and make sure we never fail in this way again. Failure and sin, emotions and foolishness—these are the risks we came to mortality to experience, learn from, and forgive.

BACK TO THE MORNING GLORIES

I am grateful to my friend for pointing out the morning glories so I could recognize them as a weed that needed tending to. I am grateful to have learned the skills of sticking with a task until it is done, even when my back hurts and my mind is tired. But I also learned a valuable, Ecclesiastes-like lesson the morning I spent hours pulling armloads of weeds while other needed tasks were ignored: There is a time to weed and a time to refrain from weeding. Likewise, there is a time for guilt and a time to ignore obsessive, perfectionist, irrational self-recrimination.

I finally realized I had more important things to do that morning than pulling up morning glories, but it was hard to pull myself away from the pull of the weeds. It was as if the morning glories had put their tentacles around me as well, choking my agency. The longer I pulled morning glories out of my garden, the more they moved into my mind. So how did I escape the tyranny of the morning glories? I realized that I had to stop looking for them. I made a conscious and deliberate choice not to look down on that last trip in from the garbage cans, but to look instead at the beauty of the towering pines. I sent my eyes to watch for birds and squirrels in the highest branches instead of watching the ground for the distinctive shape of a certain leaf that signaled my enemy was near. I focused on the mountains and not the weeds until I got myself safely into the house and back to work on other, more valuable projects.

I still pull up the morning glories, one armload at a time, but I have also learned that refusing to spend all my time pulling weeds doesn't make me selfish or lazy. It just gives me time to plant flowers, which renews my soul.

SUMMARY

What do you have a tendency to get preoccupied with to an unhealthy extent?

What worries or beliefs support your preoccupations?

How do these ideas interfere with self-forgiveness for you?

What could you tell yourself instead in order to move out of Distrust toward Self-forgiveness and Self-acceptance?

9

SELF-DESTRUCTIVE UNSELFISHNESS

*If you put a small value upon yourself, rest assured that
the world will not raise your price.*

—ANONYMOUS

We find meaning and satisfaction in sacrificing, conquering
problems, and enduring courageously—virtues of inestimable worth.
When taken to unhealthy extremes, however, these virtues turn into
impediments to self-forgiveness and self-acceptance. When we come
to depend on suffering to feel better about ourselves, deflect others'
demands, or barter for love—often without fully realizing what we
are doing—our "unselfishness" can become self-destructive. We hold
on to self-blame, self-abasement, or exaggerated restitution to others
in a mistaken effort to gain self-respect, ward off others' anger, or
earn God's love. We live in the Distrust box, never fully forgiving
or accepting ourselves despite our generosity to others.

When we rely on self-punishment and self-blame to demonstrate "character" or "earn" love, we may doubt the value of self-forgiveness even though we also desire it. Sorting this out gets tricky because self-destructive unselfishness works only if we don't see it clearly. Once recognized, the pattern of hurting ourselves to show we deserve love no longer feels so noble, and self-flagellation to appease the angry gods no longer comforts us. However, even when we catch on to what we are doing, we can't always see another way to meet our genuine needs for approval, protection, or care. We get used to overdoing service, sacrifice, or endurance to the point of unnecessary deprivation or self-harm, and we don't really trust that we can meet our needs in other ways.

Let's consider some concrete examples of self-destructive unselfishness to get a better handle on what it might look like:

+ Peg would love to attend a glass-blowing class she sees advertised, but she is afraid her teenagers will not get their homework done if she is not there to supervise. Peg is also nervous about spending family funds on such a frivolous interest. Peg's husband is a good provider and her children do well in school. Peg's principal "self-indulgence" is investing in supplies for cute charts and activities for her Primary class. Peg keeps looking at the ad but never signs up.

+ Devon's parents are committed Catholics, and when Devon joined The Church of Jesus Christ of Latter-day Saints his parents were angry and deeply hurt. His dad is an alcoholic who won't admit he has a problem, and his mother is not far behind. They find Devon's new standards on alcohol ridiculous, and they expect Devon to keep his ideas on drinking to himself. Devon frets about the grief he has caused his parents, but he also hates being around them and generally keeps his distance. He assuages his guilt by loaning his parents money they never pay back, making excuses for his dad to his dad's boss and being willing to pick his dad up at any time of the day or night when he calls from a bar needing a ride home.

+ Shannon loves to buy gifts that others really enjoy, and she spends a lot of time and effort on selecting presents for her siblings and their families at Christmas. She also works hard to stay connected with them by e-mail, invites them over regularly for meals, and supports their children's activities. Neither her brother nor her sister reciprocates this attention in ways that are meaningful to Shannon. They often do things together as families without including Shannon, give her gift certificates for Christmas, and get annoyed when Shannon complains about feeling left out. Shannon hopes that if she just tries a little harder to please them her siblings will eventually appreciate what a good person she is and see how much they hurt her with their indifference.

When otherwise reasonable people consistently indulge others at their own expense, permit unfair treatment, let others take advantage of them, or allow emotional or physical abuse, it is hard for onlookers to understand. Why would such a nice, rational person allow such treatment? Stay with such a loser boyfriend? Put up with such an unreasonable boss? Talk so negatively of herself? Keep doing so much and getting so little?

Some do it for much the same reason that we pay good money to watch Rocky Balboa get beat up in the boxing ring or (for women who think they are off this hook) watch Anne Hathaway being strung along in the emotional slugfest of *The Devil Wears Prada*. The fact is, pain is part of life, sometimes a fascinating part of life, and there is a certain perverse pleasure for all of us in experiencing it, watching it, and conquering it. But we also sign up for the short end of the stick again and again because at some level it solves a problem for us, even though we may not be fully aware of how. That lack of awareness can leave us confused and confined by our choices. We are left wondering what we did to deserve such abuse, while others wonder why we can't see that we are doing it to ourselves.

WHY *DO* WE DO IT?

We generally overdo unselfishness to try to (1) gain love that we think comes only with pain, (2) demonstrate moral superiority, or (3) earn appreciation and respect to boost our self-esteem. Let's look at these in more detail.

First, self-destructive unselfishness is often underscored by the deep belief that only when we are hurting, sacrificing, or paying attention to others' needs over our own do we deserve love and attention. We basically try to buy love and care we don't think we deserve otherwise by being indispensable. The less powerful members of any society, family, or group often learn to overattend to others in an effort to deserve protection or care. Children who have been excessively blamed or hurt in the past by people they depended on for survival often expect connection to always come in a mixed bag that also includes being used, criticized, devalued, or left unprotected. When essential relationships have come in the ugly gift wrap of abuse, seduction, or neglect, or when most of the attention we got as kids was somehow connected with being hurt or humiliated, then hurt and humiliation will feel familiar and even necessary for us to get love. Hurtful connection beats no connection, and suffering may even give us the illusion of feeling engaged and alive instead of lonely and dead inside.

Since almost all of us were both caressed and paddled by the same hand, all of us to some degree see pain as a part of closeness. For some, however, this connection is tragic and self-destructive. For adults, extreme unselfishness in relationships can deter growth in both the giver and receiver. We don't grow because we don't get to feel loved as an equal but only tolerated as a servant. The other person doesn't grow because he is allowed to treat a fellow human unfairly and believe he deserves it. When we use unselfishness to earn appreciation, relief from overwork, or protection that never materializes, we may need to reconsider our tactics.

Second, some of us overdo self-sacrifice to demonstrate moral superiority. We keep coming back to an abusive spouse because it makes us feel saintly to be so forgiving and benevolent. We put up with unreasonable work demands because we feel needed, valuable, and just a little more righteous than the lazy, immature boss we are dealing with. We berate ourselves for a terrible piano solo others are complimenting to show our superior humility (now there's an oxymoron) and high standards. We allow others to get away with being irresponsible so we can be the responsible one. We tolerate pain or even self-inflict it in an effort to demonstrate our long-suffering ("You can see how awful my wife is and what a saint I must be to live with her"), invoke help ("If I give you everything you ask and more, surely you will finally see my worth to you and do something for me in return"), or seek relief from blame or hurt ("I was such a terrible, awful mother that I can hardly stand myself, so don't make me feel worse by telling me your problems"). Needless to say, self-forgiveness and self-acceptance won't come easily when we depend on self-blame and professed inferiority to feel good about ourselves.

Third, we may believe that we can earn appreciation and esteem only if we submissively overserve. When we depend on others' appreciation to keep us from feeling invisible and inferior, we will do almost anything to get it. We serve and serve, not realizing we are setting others up to take us for granted, resent us for having any needs of our own, and expect us to take care of them. After all, isn't that what we seem to promise when we ask so little for ourselves? In fact, we may actually goad others into behaving badly by the subtle ways we irritate, invade, ignore, criticize, *neeeed*, or patronize them—all the while thinking we are the ones giving, giving, giving.

In all three of these situations, we don't see the subtle ways we set ourselves up for hurt, so we can't figure out why life keeps dumping on us. Are we really just the undeserving, selfish children we were told we were—or are we really more humble, selfless, and noble than the people who take advantage of us? Part of us believes one thing; part believes the other. Deep in our heart of hearts we know we aren't really that bad, but we also fear we are because somehow we know our unselfishness is not entirely unselfish. We provoke indifference and self-centeredness in others; then we even the scales by acting out in selfish and provocative ways, feeling we deserve something back for all we do. When we finally stand up for ourselves we may do it irresponsibly or sneakily, compounding our confusion about whether we really are or are not selfish and undeserving.

RESENTMENT

Feelings of resentment are my cue that I'm overdoing self-destructive unselfishness and acting like a martyr. While those on the shame-pride continuum may feel resentful when lesser mortals get in their way or they have to do work they don't like, the self-destructively unselfish do things they resent to demonstrate how much more they do than others or how deserving they are of appreciation. I've learned over the years to see my resentment as a red flag on a sign that reads, "Road Closed Ahead." When I do things with a sigh that communicates my resentment rather than negotiate more directly for what is fair, I'm copping out of real dialogue and opting instead to feel morally superior to those I think pick on me—but still letting them pick on me. While we all have to do some things we don't want to, when a lot of resentment accompanies our behavior we may not be acting out of charity or even necessity but manipulation. Using icy, martyr-tinged resentment to guilt-trip others into appreciating us or doing what we want sets us up for a backlash of anger, resistance, and frustration.

Most of us know what it feels like to be resentfully guilt-tripped into doing what someone else wants, and it doesn't feel very good. When another person is stewing in self-pity, we almost feel justified in putting up a fight or taking advantage of him. We resent his resentment. We don't think we have a fair chance of being heard, and we are in no mood to hear him. Even if we are the soft-hearted kind who takes the bait, feels sorry for him, and does what he expects, eventually we start wondering if he can really be as powerless and victimized as he appears. Our genuine feelings of charity and empathy yield to feelings of annoyance over having been used. Even if we feel guilty on cue for not helping out or not responding to a request, we also feel angry and unsympathetic. Our guilty feelings do not promote change but rather self-justification and blame of the other person for his unfair expectations.

We know this, and yet we still yield to the temptation to make others feel guilty by resentfully doing what they certainly should understand is really *their* responsibility. I think it is probably a sin to make people feel guilty just to get our way, especially when their guilt is not likely to produce real repentance but rather resistance to change. We are in essence teaching others to ignore their guilty feelings because they know they have been manipulated, instead of teaching them to pay attention to legitimate guilty feelings as a signal of the need to repent.

Unfortunately, even if we have learned by repeated experience how bad it feels to be guilt-tripped, we may not know a better way. Perhaps we've tried asking nicely and were ignored, so we up the ante by nagging or complaining. Finally we just give up and do it ourselves—resentfully. Or maybe someone else flatly asks us to do more and more, and when we try to point out this unfairness, the person doesn't back off. When someone pushes hard enough or angrily enough, we break down and do what we're asked—resentfully.

If it sounds like I know a lot about this it is because I do, and not from clinical training. But I have also learned that resentfully playing martyr is like cheating on our homework—it may get us what we want but not fairly and not with our honor or self-respect intact. There is no good substitute for calmly stating what we want and need and fairly listening to another person about how what that person needs is different. This means we have to listen honestly and thoughtfully, and to request honestly and thoughtfully, so that we can help each other get the problem solved and the job done. It may also mean giving in on some of the high standards that make us feel safe, acknowledging anger without getting defensive or capitulating, and giving up some of our moral superiority for doing it all and getting nothing back.

Even with teenagers, known for their inexperience at managing the boundary between others' demands and their own self-respect (I was about to say "known for their immaturity and sneaky attempts to get out of work," but let me work a little harder at this honesty stuff), bullying them with our resentment is a false ally. True, more honest approaches will not always work either, if "work" means "coerce them into doing what we want." But natural consequences (which we often don't want to enforce for fear of relinquishing our saintly reputation) and calm, honest talk are generally more effective than guilt-trips and excessive self-sacrifice.

Like an addict who will never completely eliminate tempta-tion, I will probably always feel the pull to play martyr and induce guilt to get my way. I will probably always feel resentment some-times. But I am learning to see resentment as a cue to manage my stress and relationships differently, not as a cue to act out with self-pity and blame. If I feel resentful about something I'd like others to change, I have one of three choices: (1) just keep doing it and change my attitude by remembering the nice things the other person does for me as well; (2) keep doing it, recognizing that if I'm too chicken to bring it up honestly, this is my problem, not the other person's; or (3) tell the person what I'd like and ask her to change (not that I absolutely deserve for her to change, as any rational, thoughtful per-son would obviously see), but also say I want to listen to what she wants too. Then listen, negotiate, and find a reasonable solution. None of this is easy—with some people it may not even be possible—but it beats feeling angry, despairing, and resentful.

SELF-DESTRUCTIVE SELF-BLAME

Self-destructive unselfishness interferes with our ability to understand or receive God's forgiveness and grace, which are never tinged with humiliation, neglect, or self-interest. It is difficult to see God's forgiveness or help when we assume we can deserve them only through more self-flagellation. We're not so sure we want to sign up for love anyway when we expect it to come with punishing demands. Better to keep God and other people at a safe distance by resenting, fearing, and trying to buy them off.

But this is not how love works with God. He wants us to learn a different way. God is not moved by our exaggerated protestations of our own worthlessness or badness. He is interested in our increased capacity for genuine love. We feel more loving and more lovable when we respond to each other's honest acknowledgment of mistakes with help instead of blame. Our mutual love can grow when genuine sorrow for the harm caused others is not taken advantage of and when efforts to improve are not shamed or berated. In contrast, resentful self-blame can lock us and others into stifling roles of either overdoing or underdoing. We deny our legitimate needs and others' legitimate strengths, and we all stay stuck in unsatisfying redundancies.

AN EXAMPLE

Carlos was in a terrible car accident as a child and spent a lot of time in the hospital. Unfortunately, his parents had few emotional reserves for dealing with his needs, leaving Carlos feeling guilty for costing them money and time they didn't want to spend. When his dad gave Carlos's siblings a big chunk of free spending money to even out what had been spent on Carlos's medical care, Carlos felt ashamed that his treatment had cost so much, and he felt confused by his jealousy and resentment. He worked overtime to please his parents and relished any time they spent on him, insecure in their affection. He came to believe the only way he could really deserve a place in their lives was by being helpful and making them proud of his excellent school performance, but he also longed to feel loved and appreciated without having to work overtime. He often felt guilty and undeserving but also angry and resentful, which made him feel more guilty and undeserving.

Carlos took these same patterns to his work with a small computer start-up company, both wanting to please his boss and resenting his unrelenting demands. Carlos didn't see that he contributed to his boss's disappointment in him by not making deadlines, overfocusing on irrelevant details, and overspending his budget. Carlos could only see how much he gave up for work, even jeopardizing his health to work overtime, with little appreciation in return.

Yet Carlos did not quit his job, nor did his boss fire him. Both felt responsible to stick it out no matter how hard it was because underneath each felt sorry for the other, felt vaguely guilty for not doing a better job themselves, and privately enjoyed feeling slightly superior to the other, albeit for different reasons. Carlos had a very difficult time seeing how he could influence his boss's unfair treatment of him, and he wondered how he always managed to end up getting taken advantage of. He alternated between blaming his boss and blaming himself, not really forgiving either.

Carlos's bishop encouraged personal prayer, study, and professional counseling to help him change this deeply imbedded but self-destructive pattern. In time, Carlos gained enough genuine self-understanding and self-compassion to see the ways he sabotaged himself by expecting both too much and too little of himself and others. It was hard to admit that he contributed to these patterns—that he actually set others up to take advantage of him. He could afford to contemplate such possibilities only when his investment in scripture study and prayer helped him feel more consistently safe in God's love—and not just when he "deserved" it by punishing self-sacrifice. By gaining compassion for his injuries, empathy for his "unacceptable" feelings of anger, jealousy, and shame, and trust in God's tender understanding, he gained courage to tackle the self-destructive patterns undermining his relationships. Forgiving himself was easier once he stopped thinking self-blame proved his superior humility, or self-punishment could buy off God's anger.

FROM SELF-DESTRUCTIVE UNSELFISHNESS
TO SELF-FORGIVENESS

Because these patterns are imbedded in two-way relationships that other people may like just the way they are, reforming masochists may need a lot of support to change. Those we overserve may be quite invested in preserving patterns from which they benefit. They may not see what they lose when someone consistently overdoes for them, undermining their maturity, goodness, and strength. When the reforming martyr is also infuriating, demanding, thoughtless, or childish (which of course he or she sometimes is), it is easier to blame him or her than to see how both parties participate in the problem.

It is hard to give up the esteem-enhancing roles of giver, sacrificer, and caretaker and be happy just being an average, giving-and-taking human. It is also hard for others to give up the esteem-enhancing roles of receiver, servee, and sought-after one. But when each party can comfortably share both sets of roles, each gets to grow through both serving and receiving.

CHALLENGING OUR VIEW OF GOD

If you see yourself in any of the above, you can begin to seek positive change with God, yourself, and others. First, challenge your image of a punishing, demanding god who will be close or caring only if you hurt. The part of you reading this sentence may not think of God this way at all, but chances are the part of you that dwells on how bad you are does. Most of us have multiple images of God in our minds, though we may not realize it. Some of these images coincide with God's true nature as we experience Him when we are closest to the Spirit. Others are false images tainted by experiences with caretakers or authority figures. One of our mortal challenges is to tease these two sets of images apart, holding on to the true God, the loving Father we sense when we are closest to the Spirit.

When we are not so close, we get tempted to return to faulty images of a punishing, critical god who needs to be appeased with our suffering. While we marvel at how quickly the ancient Israelites turned to idols, we have exactly the same challenge—but the false idols we are tempted to worship take form in our minds, not with our hands. Our challenge is to patiently wait for the Spirit's return while trusting in God's love, goodness, and timing—rather than adopt false views of an indifferent or punishing god who will only be appeased with our self-loathing. Self-acceptance and self-forgiveness are possible only when we trust God to be forgiving and accepting.

CHALLENGING OUR VIEW OF OURSELVES

We can also monitor how we think about ourselves when we are stressed or lonely. Do we use anger with ourselves to beat others to the punch so that we are not surprised by their hurtful comments? Do we berate ourselves to show we are more humble than others? Do we ignore people's legitimate complaints while focusing only on how unappreciative they are of all we do? If the answer to these questions is yes, we can learn to talk to ourselves in more honest, productive ways.

For example, let's revisit the experience of Carlos, whose story is told above. He insisted that his whole goal in life was to keep his boss happy, despite the man's insatiable demands—yet Carlos was often undependable, overfocused on things that weren't important to his boss at all, and resistant to some of his boss's legitimate expectations. Carlos began to see that as painful as his work situation felt at times, it supported his self-esteem by making him feel superior to his unreasonable employer. At the same time, he actually called the shots about how he would overperform in some areas and underperform in others, sneaking around his boss's efforts to control him.

As Carlos began to acknowledge these patterns more openly, he began to take a hard look at the shaky self-esteem that seemed to underpin them. He began to notice when he based his self-worth on hurting more than others, sacrificing more than others, and serving more than others. Carlos began to wonder if he was setting himself up to be taken advantage of because at some level it worked for him. For example, he saw that he could avoid taking his boss's complaints seriously by focusing instead on his own sacrifices and boundless efforts. He could blame his problems on how unfairly life treated him instead of doing the very hard work of trying to change.

At first Carlos just felt embarrassed to see himself in this new light, but he could also see how his worldview had made sense in his childhood, even though it kept him stuck now. As he focused on the love and patience he occasionally felt from the Lord, he gained courage to look more honestly at his life. He began to wonder if in his search for simple appreciation he had actually been teaching people to take advantage of him, ignore him, and criticize him, just as his parents had. It was almost as if he didn't quite know who he was without these problems to push against. But he became interested in finding out. He began to imagine that self-forgiveness and self-acceptance might be worth a try, even though they might require real change as well as real humility instead of his current patterns of slavish overdoing in some areas while ignoring legitimate expectations in other areas.

CHALLENGING OUR VIEW OF RELATIONSHIPS

As we blame others less for their excessive expectations and blame ourselves less for disappointing them, our relationships with others can begin to change. Although it can feel pointless and even dangerous to ask for what we need in a calm, straightforward fashion, this is an important skill to develop. It takes practice to listen without defensiveness, ask without whining, insist without anger, and stay connected in the face of disagreement, but these skills help us create more equitable and loving relationships.

When we give up the role of martyr and both give and expect fair, respectful treatment, the initial reaction from others will often be annoyance and frustration, not delighted adjustment. No one likes to have the familiar rules of a relationship changed unexpectedly, especially if they think they benefit from the current ones. But if we can stay both connected and clear in our new position, our relationship can begin to become more honest, equitable, and real.

Harriet Goldhor Lerner, author of *The Dance of Anger*,[1] tells of a woman who had registered for a presentation Lerner was making. When the woman's husband was not supportive of her decision, she called to tell Lerner that she couldn't attend. She told Lerner that she had gotten really, really angry with her husband about his disapproval but to no avail. Lerner notes that the woman's anger, while it appeared to be an effort to stand up for herself, was really a substitute for self-affirming action. Her anger gave her the illusion of strength and courage while in actuality it kept her from addressing her husband's concerns or taking responsibility for her own decisions. While appropriate feelings of anger can help mobilize us to right wrongs and enact our beliefs, loud displays of anger just give us the illusion of effectiveness while nothing really changes. In fact, angry displays are not nearly as effective as calm clarity, genuine listening and empathy, and consistent follow-through on our choices.

Lerner points out that change is always a complicated matter, however. Our self-destructive behavior may look foolish to outsiders, but when we believe other people control the lifeboat and will permit us aboard only if we keep rowing as hard as we can, we are justifiably cautious about asking them to take a turn with the oars. It makes sense to be thoughtful and cautious about our change efforts so we do not sabotage ourselves by trying too much too fast and before we have thought through the implications. It takes more courage to ask thoughtful questions of ourselves and others, clarify positions and values, consider options, and take small steps at a time than to stage a dramatic showdown.

There is certainly a time for unselfishness, self-sacrifice, and patience with the faults of others. Paul's definition of charity evokes images of long-suffering and selfless humility (1 Corinthians 13:4–7). But Paul also says, "Though I bestow all my goods to feed the poor, and though I give my body to be burned, and have not charity, it profiteth me nothing" (v. 3). In other words, even when we act unselfishly, even when we suffer deprivation or volunteer for pain, if we are acting out of something other than genuine charity it doesn't do us any lasting good. Self-destructive unselfishness is not charity. It is motivated instead by insecurity and the fear of not being important enough to keep. True charity is steeped in compassion and equality, not self-hatred, fear of abandonment, or trying to prove our real merit by being lowlier than others.

There is a fine line between self-affirming unselfishness and self-destructive unselfishness. Some of the most delightful, kind, generous people I know walk that line. Strengths and weaknesses generally are flip sides of the same coin, and the very qualities that we disdain in people who let others walk all over them are attractive when we are the beneficiaries of their generosity. But when unselfishness becomes self-destructive, no one really benefits in the long run. Resentment builds, people are coddled in weaknesses, and the score is eventually evened in sneaky ways. While the self-destructively unselfish person may imagine she is earning her way to forgiveness, she may only be locking herself into a worldview that precludes letting it in. Genuine self-forgiveness and self-acceptance follow from the deep self-respect that comes from trusting God's love, valuing ourselves equally with others, and taking correction gracefully.

SUMMARY

What things do you do that you resent?

What might be an honest way to handle those things?

What are some characteristics you sometimes assign to God that are not consistent with the image of a loving, patient, kind, generous Father?

How would you describe the God you know from your most spiritual experiences?

What would be scary about giving up the idea of earning love through self-sacrifice or suffering?

10

TRAUMA AND ABUSE

*In the world ye shall have tribulation: but be of good
cheer; I have overcome the world.*

JOHN 16:33

At about 4:15 P.M. on July 15, 1976, a school bus with twenty-six
children, ages five to fourteen, inexplicably disappeared somewhere
between its third and fourth stop along rural Avenue 21 in
Chowchilla, California.[1] Hours later the bus was found in a drainage
ditch hidden under debris, but the children and driver were gone. In
the flurry of calls and media interest that followed, the local police
phone lines were so jammed that the three kidnappers—men in
their early twenties from prosperous families—were unable to get
through to make their demand for $5 million in ransom. Meanwhile,
they loaded the bus driver and the children at gunpoint into two
vehicles. They drove circuitously for eleven hours to a rock quarry
one hundred miles away, where they had previously buried an old
moving van several feet underground. At about 3:00 A.M. they low-
ered the children and bus driver into the buried moving van, which

was scantily supplied with food, water, and some old mattresses; then they left them in the dark.

After about twelve hours underground, the bus driver and some of the older boys successfully piled up the mattresses so they could climb up to the battened-down top corner from which they had entered their buried prison. After four hours of frustrating effort they succeeded in wedging the cover open, despite two heavy industrial batteries securing it. They were able to create a small opening through which the children and then their driver escaped at dusk into the almost deserted quarry. Physically and emotionally exhausted, they eventually found some quarry workers, who called the police. The children were loaded onto another bus, and thirty-six hours after their abduction they were returned to their families.

The three kidnappers were apprehended within two weeks, but their court proceedings strung on for almost eighteen months. In the end, all three men were sentenced to life in prison; as of this writing all three are still serving their sentences. The judge who tried the case determined that even though the children were not physically injured, the extent of emotional trauma they sustained constituted bodily harm. Mental health workers who followed the children over several years noted such symptoms as nightmares, extreme anxiety, hopelessness about ever having a happy or normal life, certainty that something similar would happen again, trouble in school, and physical disorders. Four years after the abduction, one nine-year-old girl had virtually not grown an inch. But all of the children stopped growing in other ways, their emotional maturation stunted by their terrifying experience.

Thankfully, relatively few people are subjected to kidnapping and abandonment in a sealed underground hole. Unfortunately, other forms of physical, sexual, or emotional abuse or trauma are more common, arresting emotional growth and well-being. Children are especially vulnerable to these injuries and can suffer long-term changes in how their brains and emotions develop. They are more prone to depression, anxiety, learning difficulties, relationship problems, and physical maladies not only in the immediate aftermath of the trauma but also over the course of years.

Pertinent to our subject, victims of trauma or abuse can also have exaggerated problems with self-forgiveness. They may experience traumatic shame, may try to prevent further trauma through unwarranted self-blame, or may see turning back the clock as the only way to find peace. Each of these has implications for self-forgiveness. Let's consider them in more detail.

TRAUMATIC SHAME

Shame is a common feeling for victims of trauma or abuse. There is something shameful about being powerless, not having had the foresight or strength to keep from getting hurt. When other people have deliberately inflicted harm upon us, this feeling of shame is intensified. We may feel diminished and stupid for being less than others and subject to their will. Our feelings of shame may lead us to falsely believe that the trauma occurred as a result of our wrongdoing.

Feelings of shame can be intensified by the justifiable anger that comes on the heels of injustice. We may feel ashamed about the enormity of this anger. Onlookers who are afraid of angry displays may communicate disapproval or tell us we are overreacting, adding to our experience of being outside of the norm. Feeling thus isolated and misunderstood contributes to our feelings of shame. We may conclude that our reactions of anger or fear are unjustified or unusual instead of a natural result of an experience most other people just have not had.

Other people may also distance themselves from the chaos and uncertainty that trauma or abuse imply, not wanting to believe that such things could also happen to them. When others recoil from us, we are left holding the bag of shame alone. Trauma turns us into outsiders and can make us feel rejected from human society. We can have the sensation of being punished or disgraced simply because something terrible happened to us that others cannot fully understand.

Shame is also a common experience for *witnesses* of trauma or abuse, even if they were not directly injured. We may feel shame for not having been able to prevent the trauma or respond to it appropriately. We may not understand that witnessing violence or trauma is in itself an assault on our sense of safety and normalcy, and that we too are victims.

We may also feel ashamed when we overreact to something bad happening to someone we don't know, or don't know that well. If we have not connected the current event to the old wounds it stirs up in us, we may wonder why we are reacting so strongly. Others may also wonder, thinking we are exaggerating for effect. We feel ashamed.

Survivors may also feel shame or guilt for not having suffered as much as others who were not spared. We feel a natural relief when we are lucky enough not to have been hurt or killed. But our compassion for others also makes us feel guilty for escaping while others suffered. We may wonder if they blame us. We can't see how we deserved to go unscathed—any more than they deserved to be hurt. This awareness may turn our attention to our faults and flaws and the other person's innocence as we try to restore order and fairness to an incoherent world.

Traumatic shame, though common, is an inaccurate measure of what is fair or real about our responsibility for wrongdoing. Some people will wrongly conclude that traumatic shame is a reliable indicator of real guilt and will go looking for faults to justify their feelings. Others will manage feelings of shame by finding someone else to blame, sidestepping the need to deal with the shame directly in order to dispel it. Traumatic shame contributes to feelings of self-recrimination and impedes self-forgiveness, especially when we don't recognize it for what it is. When we recognize shame as a normal response to trauma but not an accurate indicator of wrongdoing, we can avoid faulty conclusions about what the shame means.

THE SEARCH FOR CONTROL

While onlookers can understand a victim struggling to forgive a perpetrator, it is less clear why victims would have trouble forgiving themselves, or even what they would think they need to forgive themselves for. Yet the need to regain the sense of control that trauma or abuse has stolen sends us looking for what we did wrong to bring this problem upon ourselves. After all, if we are responsible for what happened, we can exercise control to make sure it doesn't happen again. To let go of self-blame can feel like relinquishing this precarious sense of control.

For example, Marilyn was eight when her father was killed in a terrible car accident. She still remembers thinking that if she had only managed to break her leg earlier that day, her father would have been in the hospital with her instead of on the road when the accident occurred. Falsely believing she was at fault helped her not blame God for taking her father, protecting her young faith in God's goodness and the world's fairness. Her self-sacrificing wish was an effort, however futile, to regain some sense of control over this terrible loss. Sadly, this effort backfired, not helping the situation at all and leaving Marilyn feeling guilty for not having managed to break her leg to save her father's life. Yet similar thinking is common in both children and adults in the aftermath of traumatic loss.

Stacy, a client who had been sexually abused at age nine by a family member, thought she had put her life together reasonably well as an adult. She had raised a good family, served in the Church, and worked extremely hard to be a good person. Too hard, in fact. Only at midlife did the price of her overanxious conscientiousness begin to hit home. As she realized with sudden clarity that deep self-doubt underscored her exaggerated efforts to be good, she realized she had blamed herself for what had happened when she was a child. The realization that she had built her life around proving her innocence jolted her. But instead of feeling relief from this burden of unwarranted guilt, she wondered tearfully, "It is excruciating to think this might really have been my fault, that I could have stopped it—so why would I think something so awful unless it is true?"

Interviews with the children kidnapped in Chowchilla provide insight to Stacy's question. A psychiatrist who followed the case over several years found that 73 percent of the children believed they had received some prior warning about the event but had ignored it or misunderstood its significance. Several of them misremembered things that had actually happened after the kidnapping, believing they had happened beforehand as an omen. Others found significance in unrelated events that they came to believe had been forewarnings. This belief helped the children bring order and predictability to the chaos they had experienced, giving them some way to imagine a level of control they did not actually have. After all, if they could have prevented the kidnapping by paying more attention to warnings, then surely they could prevent a future repeat by being more vigilant next time. Psychotherapists notice similar thinking in victims of abuse. Stacy falls into this category.

Children seem to come prewired to search for cause-and-effect relationships among events. We are predisposed from birth to try to figure out how the world works so we can exercise agency to maneuver within it. Predictability and routine teach us what to expect and how to stay safe. When something unexpected and dangerous happens, our brains work overtime to figure out what caused it so we can make sure it does not happen again. If we can find a cause, especially one we can control, we have a way to prevent a recurrence. This diminishes our sense of threat in a nonsensical and dangerous world.

If adults often follow this flawed logic, children are even more prone to do so. They lack sophisticated reasoning skills, and they depend too heavily on adults to face the possibility that adults can harm them without provocation. It is less frightening for a child to believe that bad things happened because the child provoked them or ignored warnings than to believe that adults, social organizations, or heavenly powers looked to for safety are *that* crazy, powerless, or unpredictable. Blaming self is a way to hold on to some illusion of control in a world turned upside down.

Of course, pretending control over such massive events is not unilaterally comforting. Thus, children and adults who blame themselves may in the next moment angrily and vehemently blame others. The powerful perpetrators, caretakers, or authority figures who control their destinies are seen as bigger than life, idealized and invested with enormous power. There is little room for compassion or empathy for mitigating circumstances or human failure when we perceive these other people's power as being so out of proportion with our own. This leaves us with a burden of blame that is as difficult to forgive in others as in ourselves.

STUCK IN THE PAST

In addition to traumatic shame and the search for control, many victims of trauma develop a skewed relationship with time. For some of the Chowchilla children, every minute in the buried moving van felt like hours; for others, the hours all blurred together. It was difficult for investigators to piece together the timing of events because the children remembered the passing of time so differently. Some wanted to hold time still lest something worse should happen next. Others wanted to rush it along, hoping to get out of the tension of terrible uncertainty.

All the children reported that their moments of greatest terror occurred whenever they were moved to a new location—from the bus to the transport vehicles, from the vehicles to the buried moving van, or when escaping their underground prison. Most were even terrified of getting into the bus that would take them home after they were rescued—not so much because it reminded them of the bus from which they were abducted but simply because any change or transition felt terribly threatening. In the midst of this trauma, their instinct was to put on the brakes, make no decision until the last possible moment, stop time.

Our sense of time is altered by trauma. The world seems to shift on its axis when something so upending occurs. Nothing is ever quite the same again. If we are not securely attached to our caretakers, if others do not help us make sense out of the trauma and weave it into a coherent story, or if we have already experienced other traumatic events, we will be even more likely to feel that the only way to make the world right again is to somehow turn back time and undo the horrible thing that happened. All of our energy goes into somehow being angry enough, saintly enough, desperate enough, or—pertinent to our subject—penitent enough to get the universe to rewind itself and put things back the way they were before.

Forgiving others is untenable in part because it requires accepting the betrayal and moving forward instead of somehow finding a way to retreat to the unchallenged safety we felt before. Forgiving ourselves (assuming there is anything to forgive) is untenable for similar reasons. We don't want to cope; we want to undo.

The flashbacks and nightmares plaguing people after a trauma often reflect this effort to turn back the clock or stop time. A recurring nightmare or flashback often keeps the person repeating a moment that, for all its terror, is slightly less awful than whatever happened next. By keeping our attention focused on the terror of this image, we can avoid the even more bitter realities that followed. As terrible as it is to remember again and again the dreaded knock on the door, the moment of impact, the explosive blast, the look on someone's face, the moments that follow are worse—when the loss sinks in, the life course is forever altered, the death becomes permanent, or the betrayal fully registers. Anger at others and blaming ourselves become our desperate ways to hold on to the false hope that it can all be undone, that we can have the care, protection, safety, help, or control we needed and did not have, and without which our world has been irrevocably changed. Yet changes in the brain following abuse or neglect are enduring, leading to heightened sensitivity to threat and long-term difficulty with self-soothing. If our attachments to parents or caretakers are weak, smaller traumas have bigger impact.

REDEMPTION VERSUS PREVENTION

The adversary's plan focused on prevention—saving us all by not allowing problems in the first place. It is the plan the traumatized child or adult longs for in the moment of betrayal or loss. Put the cat back in the bag and never allow for the possibility of its escape.

Then, maybe, I can feel safe again. But this is not the plan we sustained in the heavenly councils—or the plan we must choose to sustain again and again throughout life if we are to make our way from the secure safety of Eden across the flatlands of mortality and on to a world of celestial wisdom and power. God's great plan of happiness and salvation requires submission to the demands of living in irreversible time where cause-and-effect relationships can unfold, thus permitting the exercise of human agency. There is no turning back the clock, no wresting of control over other people's choices. In fact, these would destroy the agency that allows us power, learning, and growth.

There is, however, redemption. This is why the whole plan of salvation hinges on the atonement of Jesus Christ.

A STORY

While the scriptures are filled with stories of people traumatizing one another, Abraham's story in the Pearl of Great Price is particularly poignant for me. His father not only turns to the worship of idols but also seeks to sacrifice Abraham on an altar. Idolatrous priests of Pharaoh, whose religion predominated even in this distant land of Ur, had already sacrificed three sisters who would not yield their virtue in the worship of these false Egyptian gods. Abraham stated that the priests had also "laid violence upon me, that they might slay me also" (Abraham 1:12). He was strapped onto the altar of sacrifice, spared by God only when the priests' hands were lifted in the final intention of murder.

While not all victims of violence are so spared, only those who live to tell the tale endure the ongoing emotional effects of their experience. Abraham was not spared the threat of a violent death, the reality of physical injury, or the dark betrayal of his father. Only when he was about to die did God intervene. The angels who pre-serve our lives are not always visible or credited for protecting us. While we may sometimes think we would prefer death to the insanity of life after trauma, God may have purposes and perspec-tive that see beyond our current suffering. God's tender words to Abraham speak of both His rescuing hand and a future of hope and challenge:

> Abraham, Abraham, behold, my name is Jehovah, and I have heard thee, and have come down to deliver thee, and to take thee away from thy father's house, and from all thy kinsfolk, into a strange land which thou knowest not of.
>
> And this because they have turned their hearts away from me . . . ; therefore I have come down to visit them, and to destroy him who hath lifted up his hand against thee, Abraham, my son, to take away thy life.
>
> Behold, I will lead thee by my hand, and I will take thee, to put upon thee my name, even the Priesthood of thy father, and my power shall be over thee (Abraham 1:16–18).

I don't know if the idea of taking off for a new land was comforting or frightening to Abraham—maybe some of both. God's promise to Abraham of a new Father, a new hand to replace the hands raised against him, a new name and priesthood, and a new inheritance—these are His promises to all the faithful. We are the children of Abraham: victims of the godlessness of the world and, if we will choose it, gathered under the healing wing of Jehovah.

Abraham's idolatrous father repented for a time when a sore famine afflicted the entire land. He even followed Abraham as the Lord led him away. We wonder how Abraham felt about his father, who had previously sought his life, tagging along on this journey. His

father's repentance was short-lived: when they reached a more prosperous country, he chose to stay and returned to his idolatry. When
God led Abraham and his family on, famine closing in as they jour-
neyed among idolatrous people, Abraham built an altar and prayed
that his father would be preserved from the famine. Abraham found
the rare maturity to move beyond bitterness and victimization to
pray for his enemy.

Abraham, whose father had sought to kill him, became the
father of the faithful, the great patriarch, by taking Jehovah as his
Father and God. He received the hand God offered him, accepting
the difficult journey forward rather than trying to turn back time.
He got on the bus home, even though it took him on a circuitous
and dangerous route through enemy territory. Having experienced
the saving hand of Jehovah, he trusted the True and Living God to
take him safely home again, no matter the difficulties of the journey
or its ultimate outcome (Abraham 1–2).

THE PATH OF REDEMPTION

Abraham doesn't give us a lot of detail about the healing process
after trauma, but we gather that it has much to do with coming to
deeply trust God and accept the perils inherent in mortality. It is
often difficult for us to trust the God we think abandoned us to a
terrible fate, not always seeing the full vision of how He also spared
us and leads us still. Surely God deeply understands our dilemma.
But He does not try to mollify us with false promises of safety or
ease. In fact, Satan is the one who pretends he will keep us safe from
all who would molest or threaten us. God tells us plainly that we will
surely die and that life will continue to be hard. But He also promises us that life will yield great learning, growth, even joy, and will
ultimately have been worth its most horrible downsides as we

choose the path of redemption—the path of giving and receiving forgiveness through the atonement of Christ.

Coming to deeply accept our own humanity is also part of our healing. We forgive ourselves as we both acknowledge the limits of our power and control and renounce the shame such powerlessness induces. By relinquishing our illusions of control, we also gain real understanding of our reliance on the Atonement and Resurrection. God cannot always give us what we want—escape from trauma or abuse—but He has provided all we need to make the risks of mortality worth taking.

Studies of how people cope with trauma conclude that trauma is not universally devastating. When people in stressful or abusive situations find ways to successfully cope with their struggle and receive social support, they generally heal. People who find a way out, tell others, and are believed, comforted, and helped can come to very different conclusions about their power and safety than those who do not have such support. Great resources are found in the healing stories, hopeful doctrines, and loving communities of the gospel. We can heal from trauma. But trauma will generally leave a scar.

WOUNDS TO SCARS

During bouts with asthma and pneumonia in my youth, I coughed violently at times, trying to expel the congestion that threatened my ability to breathe. With proper medication and care I surmounted these assaults to my well-being. The wounds inside my lungs gradually turned to scars, and I stopped coughing up blood. For a while this scar tissue had a noticeable impact on my lung capacity, but I no longer notice it much. Scars are not pretty, but they are definitely better than wounds. They attest to our capacity to heal.

Just as medical science is finding more and more reliable tools to help us heal from trauma's physical effects, psychology is finding more reliable tools for helping people heal from the wounds inside our psyche. As we gently reconsider the faulty conclusions we came to in the aftermath of trauma, reassociate with our body's sensations and feelings, and renegotiate a more realistic trust in God, the world, and ourselves, we begin to heal. It takes time and proper treatment to help our wounds turn to scars, and even then our scars may interfere with our normal life. Our scars will never look as pretty as our unmarred, innocent souls. But scars attest to our participation in the battle of good and evil, the battle for agency, and our right to celestial wisdom and power. We share our scars with the Savior, with whose stripes we are healed.

I couldn't summarize the available tools for treating asthma and pneumonia in a few pages, nor could I summarize the tools for treating trauma. One tool that some people find helpful in sorting through abuse or trauma is to allow their inner parts to dialogue with each other. We often talk of the mixed feelings we have about an issue by saying, "One part of me thinks this, while another part of me thinks that." Sometimes it helps to clarify these different voices, which are like different roles played by different parts of our mind. The part of us that remembers being hurt may not want to forgive the part of us that has hurt others. The part of us that is strong or tried to protect us may not want to forgive or accept the part of us that is weak. The part of us that holds our pain may not want to forgive the part that has warm feelings for someone who also hurt us. It can help to ask ourselves: What part of me won't or can't forgive what other part? What would that unforgiving part need to feel safer? As we negotiate among these parts of ourselves we restore sovereignty to our truest self, facilitating self-forgiveness.

A trained therapist is usually the best person to help us if we have been seriously traumatized and are still suffering. As we heal we can begin to identify and work to get (not just wait for) what we needed in the past but did not receive. We can develop our resources and learn not to overinvest in self-protection. We can begin to work toward understanding and even forgiving those who have damaged us, which will generally go hand in hand with greater self-forgiveness. Forgiving others does not mean saying nothing bad really happened or that we are wrong and the other person is right. Alma 42:25 reminds us that mercy cannot rob justice, and in the same way, forgiveness cannot rob truth. We are owed a debt that the perpetrator cannot repay, but Christ can, although not always in this life. As we turn the fate of the debtor to Him, we gain the right to ask God to repay us for what our debtor stole. As we increase our faith and trust in the Lord, we gain confidence that in His time and on His terms we will be given full measure, pressed down and running over, for all we are due.

We deserve compassion and patience in this healing process. We also need to take responsibility for our lives in the present, learning from our experiences and making constructive decisions to go forward. If there are ways we contributed to our own victimization, we can acknowledge and correct them, secure in the promise that God is patient with our naiveté and weaknesses and does not use the hands of the unrighteous to punish us for them. We did not deserve to be traumatized or abused, *and* we can still learn from the experience. We do not have to choose one or the other.

Although Stacy concluded that her feelings of shame about being abused were not trustworthy indicators of her guilt or responsibility, she still wondered if others thought she was responsible for not stopping her perpetrator. I asked her to take a hard look at a nine-year-old child, perhaps someone in her ward, and then ask herself who might blame a child that age for letting herself be molested.

It was not a rhetorical question, for undoubtedly there are some people who would make that accusation, including some part of Stacy's mind. Stacy thought hard about this question and concluded that there were three types of people who might hold a nine-year-old responsible for stopping a sexual predator: (1) someone who had no experience with such situations, (2) someone who was simply crazy or wrong, or (3) someone who wanted to deny his own responsibility for a similar criminal act. She decided that the opinions of such people did not determine her actual guilt or innocence.

But Stacy still wondered if she really could have stopped her abuser. Maybe, despite what others thought, she did have the power to do something if she could have only had the courage or ingenuity to do so. I asked, "Then do you think you could forgive yourself for not having had that courage or that ingenuity?" This was a difficult question, one that required Stacy to give up illusions of control, irrational shame, and desires to turn back the clock and undo the past that had so affected her life. It suggested giving up the either-or, black-and-white view she clung to for exoneration. But having spent many years in various stages of trying to answer this question, bringing painful feelings to the surface and then working to understand and heal them, Stacy was finally ready to say, "Yes." She no longer needed to just undo the past, cling to control, or regain her lost innocence in order to move forward in life. She could accept herself as someone with mortal limits without blaming herself for moral failure.

I don't pretend that this is the end of Stacy's healing. She will probably revisit these questions and others repeatedly in her life. But Stacy has made important strides on the road to forgiveness and self-forgiveness—or more accurately, self-acceptance. Stacy is on the bus home.

SUMMARY

What traumas or abuses, if any, have influenced your worldview?

What self-blaming conclusions did you come to that might need to be reconsidered?

What limits of your control or power would you have to accept to forgive yourself?

Can you accept those limits?

PART 4

TRUSTING GOD

Even when we have understood correct doctrine, repented of our sins, and worked to heal the personality traits that impede our journey to self-forgiveness, obstacles to trusting God's forgiveness still remain for some. Two special cases can make it especially difficult for us to trust that we can be forgiven and can afford to forgive ourselves. These are serious sins and parenting sins, which this section will address.

If we have committed an especially serious sin, one that seems to put us outside of the realm of normal human experience, we may wonder if we can ever really rejoin the human race. And when we feel we have failed the people we love the very most, our children, we may wonder if we can ever accept our self-disappointment. Chapters 11 and 12 will help us cross these hurdles and access God's mercy and our own.

The joy and relief Alma felt when he was forgiven will still not necessarily be the new constant state for all the repentant. The concluding chapter 13 explores self-forgiveness as a choice rather than an emotion. Though we may continue to feel regret about our past sins, we can decide as an act of agency to trust in God's goodness and receive His proffered gifts of grace. Sadness about our past choices does not mean God has not forgiven us, nor does it mean we cannot forgive ourselves. Nor does it mean that joy and peace cannot also be ours.

11

THOUGH YOUR SINS BE AS SCARLET

*Thou art angry, O Lord, with this people, because they
will not understand thy mercies which thou hast bestowed
upon them because of thy Son.*

—ALMA 33:16

While ecclesiastical leaders carry the spiritual load of helping people repent of serious sin, mental health professionals often assist people to better understand their faulty thinking, relieve their troubled feelings, and change their inappropriate behavior. As a psychologist I have had the privilege of counseling both the victims and the perpetrators of serious sins. I have worked with men and women with unfaithful spouses, parents of traumatized children, people whose parents threatened to kill them when they were young, families of serious addicts, and Church members wronged by local leaders. I have also worked with the spouses who committed adultery, the adults who have abused children, the people who have aborted pregnancies, the drug and sex addicts, and the excommunicated Church leaders who seriously wronged others. In all of these cases, I have felt that I was standing on holy ground. Being allowed into the totality of another's mortal journey is a sacred experience.

As people on both sides of sin (whether victim or perpetrator) share with me how they think, the influences on their behavior, and the pain they experience, I see what we all have in common more than what separates us. I learn much from those injured by serious sin, and I learn much from those who have committed serious sin. Often these are the same people. None of the sinners I have personally worked with were the monsters we sometimes imagine when we try to distance ourselves from evil. And none of their victims deserved or desired to be betrayed, abused, or wounded. I have never doubted that God loves and weeps for them all.

It is true that many seriously sinful people are not especially sorry about what they have done, nor do they grasp the real impact of their behavior. Their capacity for empathy may have been seriously compromised. They may lack the basic self-esteem to tolerate being wrong. Or they may grossly distort the power differentials between them and those they injure, aware only of how powerless they feel, not how powerful they appear and are. I do not say this to excuse wrongdoing; other people with similar backgrounds may still make far better choices. But I think we do differ from one another in the options we can imagine in life, the compassion we can feel, and the physiological and societal circumstances that constrain us. Addiction can severely limit our agency. Physical or mental illnesses can reduce our accountability for our poor choices.

Because I work only with people who come in voluntarily for psychotherapy, I don't work with the most recalcitrant or unrepentant offenders. Still, I have also worked with people who ended up in jail or who were never caught for heinous crimes but who I still have no trouble imagining are dearly loved and deeply understood by God. I don't think that means He excuses their sins, nor should we. But I have learned to deeply care for and understand and want to help people who have done terrible things, helping me envision that God also loves me, even in my most despicable moments.

THE CHALLENGE OF "BIG" SINS

I define big sins to include anything that would jeopardize our standing in the Church. Big sins include such things as murder, adultery, child or spouse abuse, unjustified abortion, torture, extortion, theft, kidnapping, rape, and fornication. Addiction to drugs, alcohol, sex, gambling, or pornography can also have serious impact on us and on innocent people. Information in this chapter may also apply to other sins that feel so serious that we can hardly imagine being forgiven; however, we have to be careful to distinguish sin for which we are responsible from equally horrifying situations in which we are not responsible. Killing someone in an unpreventable accident, participating in a war, having a medically necessary abortion, being raped, or making a judgment call that results in serious injury to another—these are all situations that can produce lasting remorse and even shame even though they do not constitute sin.

It takes great faith to really believe that God can forgive and save us when we have done something really awful. If we had had that much faith and clarity about our relationship with God to begin with, we probably would not have done what we did, so we are left with the challenge of not only increasing our faith in God but also doing so when we feel most undeserving of His grace. What we expect from God instead of love and mercy is anger and punishment. Perhaps this is why I so appreciate the scripture quoted at the beginning of this chapter. It starts off in language the sinner expects—language about God's anger with his people because they will not understand. We expect the next words to be about not understanding the importance of obedience or not understanding His commandments or not understanding that we are going to suffer in hell if we do not repent. And so what actually comes next startles us a bit: God is angry because we don't understand His mercy, made possible to enact because of the willing sacrifice of His Son. We just don't get how much He loves us, how complete His forgiveness can be, or how much Christ gave in order to satisfy the laws of justice and gain the right to be merciful to us. That gives a whole new perspective on godly anger.

Yet there is no question that forgiving ourselves is hard when our sins are especially damaging to others, when what we took from them cannot be paid back, or when the person we wronged sees our sin as too big to forgive—all of which are common with serious sin. Innocent victims deserve to know that God "cannot look upon sin with the least degree of allowance" (D&C 1:31). Heavy consequences and sometimes punishment rightfully follow damaging, sinful behavior, and the punishment may be heavier if the person shirks responsibility for wrongdoing.

The challenge of tackling the repentance process for big sins is compounded by many questionable and even contradictory beliefs, which we would do well to carefully consider. They include:

- Only monsters do things like this, so I can't be this bad and still be worth saving.
- Only monsters do things like this, and I'm a decent person, so what I did can't really be what it appears.
- Other people did horrible things to me, so I know what horrible is—this is different.
- Other people did worse things to me, and I survived, so what is the big deal?

- If others knew what I did they would never forgive me, so how can God?
- This isn't even my fault, so why can't we all just move on?
- I can never forgive myself—hating myself keeps me from making this mistake again.
- I could forgive myself only if I thought my behavior was mostly another's fault.
- I can never make this right, so there's no point in trying.
- I could change this any time; I just don't want to.
- What I did was justified given what the other person did to me.
- What I did was necessary to get the other person to take me seriously.

All of these beliefs keep us from the one thing that will actually make things better—repenting and receiving the atonement of Christ. Only upon this step can we gain forgiveness from God, the Church, society, and other people, and so pave the way to self-forgiveness. As we review the repentance process, we see a number of places where people with very serious sins get stuck:

- It is harder to *acknowledge* our error if we believe it puts us beyond the reach of human or divine understanding.
- We may hesitate to *confess* our sin because of the serious and potentially punitive consequences of admitting guilt.
- We may have trouble *making restitution* since the consequences of serious sin are usually beyond human capacity to repair.
- We feel that we cannot *change our behavior*; for example, we know change is especially difficult if we have a serious addiction.

- We may not know how to *apologize*, especially if our apology is not welcome.
- We may not know how to *rebuild the trust* we violated, including our trust in ourselves.
- It is hard to *accept* that we have been or can be forgiven.

Let's look at these, each in turn.

ACKNOWLEDGE

Failure to acknowledge a serious sin keeps us in the quadrant of Delusion, where we don't repent and don't humble ourselves to change. Two not-so-obvious reasons keep otherwise good people from acknowledging sin. First, sins can seem to meet important needs we don't know how to get met any other way. We all need love, esteem, protection, soothing, a sense of control, and so forth, and sometimes these needs get exaggerated when we have a history of being abused or a body that is especially sensitive to anxiety and is hard to soothe. Many sinful behaviors (pornography, abuse, lying, drugs, anger, sexual acting out, and so forth) seem to provide short-cuts to meeting such needs. We may not have thought about how our sinful choice helps us feel safer, stronger, more in control, more loved, or more important, but often sin tempts us precisely because it seems to fill such hungers or soothe such fears. If we were to consciously admit that our behavior is truly sinful, we would have to face the possibility of life without this need being met. If we can't really imagine better ways to meet our needs, it will be hard to give up a sin that seems to do the trick.

Second, good people have a hard time acknowledging big sins because they wouldn't have done the wrong thing to begin with if they hadn't somehow convinced themselves it was okay: Okay because the other person had it coming. Okay because it wasn't that bad. Okay because it was actually good. Okay because it was the best choice under the circumstances. Okay because they didn't have a choice.

I used to think rationalizing meant convincing ourselves we can get away with sin or that we'll stop soon. I've learned that good people can also convince themselves that sin is not sin at all but the reasonable thing to do if people just knew the situation. Two big indicators that we may have fallen prey to this reasoning are hiding what we are doing from others and not believing trustworthy people who tell us we are wrong.

Jim got sexually involved with another employee at work when his wife was repeatedly uninterested in sex after the birth of their third child. He reports feeling disappointed and resentful that his wife "pushed him" to such a drastic step by her poor emotional connection with him. Jim's primary attention is on his spouse's disappointing behavior, not his own. As long as he sees his wife's lack of sexual interest as the cause of his choice, he abdicates his agency to choose his own moral values and regain control of his life.

Sin is not just evidence of lack of self-discipline or good values. Sin meets our legitimate needs in illegitimate ways, blinding us to the enormous damage we do in the process. It takes a mature person to own a mistake, with no excuses, while still searching out legitimate needs and finding better ways to address them. We not only have to change our behavior to repent, but we also have to change our mind—to see the damage we do for what it is, stop trying to meet our needs at the expense of another, and acknowledge that we have violated covenants and betrayed people who trusted us. This is why God gives us all the standards He does—so that when we are blinded by our fears, needs, loneliness, or shame we will have an iron rod to hold us steady. Few of us realize how vulnerable we are when we let go of that sure guide.

Having said that, I believe the measure of our character is not only in the sins we avoid but also in what we do once we see our sins in their true light and have a chance to change our mind. Do we hide away in our private world of self-justification, blaming others and focusing only on our needs—or do we step forward when God calls us into the light, acknowledge our wrongdoing, and submit to its consequences? Do we seize the opportunity for redemption that comes only upon leaving our private Eden of insisted innocence? Perhaps the truest measure of our character is how long it takes for us to be willing to see—a few minutes, a few years, or a few millennia.

If we have any doubt about our level of responsibility or the seriousness of our sin, the simplest course is to submit our choices to the scrutiny of others. Bishops, though not infallible, are set apart as judges in Israel to help us in such matters. They can look at our behavior and circumstances more objectively than we can. Scriptures, temple covenants, conference talks, and the counsel of wise, moral friends can also help us see more accurately—if we are totally honest with them before asking their counsel.

CONFESS

Confessing and forsaking big sins is especially hard because they usually have big consequences. Yet the consequences of hiding or avoiding change are even bigger and far more lasting. Confessing our sins is a necessary step in repenting, obtaining forgiveness, and forgiving ourselves. It helps us out of the quadrant of Despair, in which we feel too hopeless to change, and moves us toward the quadrant of Self-forgiveness.

King David's choices resulted in the loss of the promise of

exaltation (D&C 132:39), yet even after his most serious sin costs him exaltation, David doesn't just decide he might as well give up. Instead, David mourns over his sins, turns to God for help, and seems to try to be the best king he can be. Despite the enormity of his sin of murder and its consequences, David seeks to turn back to God and does all he can to repent of his sins of adultery and hubris. He confesses with contrition, submits to consequences, and seems to return to God with all his heart. He appears to be a man who values truth and righteousness for their own sake, a man who willingly changes and repairs what he can.

Confessing our sins to those we injure and accepting the legal or ecclesiastical consequences demonstrates our contrition and support of God's laws. Doing so helps those we hurt to know that their injury is not ignored but mourned by us and by a just God. It puts us in contact with priesthood leaders who can guide and support us through the difficult process of change. And it helps us requalify for the Spirit we lose through sin.

MAKE RESTITUTION

Restitution is a necessary part of repentance. Making restitution does not entitle us to forgiveness, but it does show that we are not benefiting from our sins at the expense of those we damaged. It sends the signal that we are truly sorry our actions hurt others. If we cannot directly pay back the person we hurt, we can pay back the larger community or other people in similar circumstances.

Breanne doesn't remember much about her childhood, but she ended up in the hospital more than once with serious, unexplained injuries. She grew up angry and looking for escape, and drugs seemed to help with both problems. One night Breanne, high herself, dared a homeless girl she'd barely met to take what proved to be a lethal dose of narcotics. When Breanne realized the girl was dead she fled in horror, never even learning the girl's name. In time, Breanne began working her way out of the drug scene, moved away, got a job, married, had children, and became a respectable wife and mother. She never told anyone about that horrible night, but twenty years later she still had vivid nightmares of handing the girl the drugs that killed her—dreams from which she awoke in terror.

Part of what makes some sins so serious is that there is no way to fully restore what our sin took away. We cannot give back another's life, virtue, health, security, or future. Although Breanne was not legally responsible for the death of this girl, she felt morally responsible. Yet she had no way to make restitution. She had cut all ties with her former life and didn't know when or even exactly where the death took place. She felt she could never forgive herself, but she desperately wanted to do something to restore some sense of peace and honor to her life. Finally she went to a therapist for help.

Breanne had a lot of compassion for the girl who died but little understanding of how her own abuse had skewed her judgment and made her vulnerable to the temptation of drugs, with all their associated problems. As Breanne worked with her therapist, she began to put the night of the death into a more coherent story that included all that had happened before and since, instead of seeing her entire life's merit reduced to a single horrible event. It took some time before Breanne could articulate that she and the girl who died were both victims of the loveless, chaotic world they had randomly come to share. Breanne realized that she could just as easily have been the one who died, as both of them had put themselves in harm's way by their previous choices. Breanne knew she could have coped with her difficulties more responsibly, but she also came to see herself with a degree of compassion.

Breanne eventually decided there were some things she could do to make restitution and that in fact she had been doing some of those things all along. She decided she could continue to love her three children and make sure they never knew the horrors of physical abuse. She could stay off drugs and help her children do the same. She further decided to make a monthly financial contribution to a homeless shelter for youth to try to help other young people in troubled circumstances. She made a point of making her home a safe and comfortable place for her kids' friends to hang out, giving special attention to those who seemed angry or vulnerable. And she took a parenting class to help her better manage her bouts of anger and frustration at home. Breanne will always feel deeply sad about what happened that terrible night, but she is beginning to imagine that it is not the defining event of her whole life.

In Leviticus 6:4, the Lord clarifies the principle of restitution: "Because he hath sinned . . . he shall restore that which he took violently away, or the thing which he hath deceitfully gotten, or that which was delivered him to keep, or the lost thing which he found." If full restitution is not possible, our righteous living, coupled with the atonement of Jesus Christ, can meet this requirement. Elder Bruce C. Hafen explains: "At [one] extreme are those who feel that repentance asks more than they can possibly give. Many of them believe they are fully responsible to compensate for their own sins. To be sure, repentance requires that transgressors make full restitution to the limit of their ability. But there are times when we *cannot* fully compensate. It is simply impossible to return stolen virtue the way one might return a stolen car. Because we lack the power to compensate fully for the effects of our transgressions, we are utterly dependent on Christ for ultimate restitution, no matter how earnest our repentance."[1]

CHANGE

While repentance literally means turning—a change of heart and mind—we demonstrate repentance through a change of behavior. Elder James A. Cullimore said:

> Someone is reputed to have asked one of the Brethren, "When is one forgiven of his transgressions?" and he replied, "When he has repented." He was then asked, "How do you know when he has repented?" His answer was, "If you could look into the heart of the individual you could tell. Possibly repentance was at the time of confession, but since we don't know, there must be a time in which the person can demonstrate his repentance through faithfulness to the gospel."[2]

In the Book of Mormon, some Lamanites who had provoked war and killed many Nephites were converted to Christ. They had a full change of heart and mind about their former behavior. They buried their weapons and made a covenant of peace they kept even at the peril of their lives, so concerned were they about not taking their forgiveness for granted. Their behavior change was radical and immediate once they had changed their minds. They were not "addicted" to killing Nephites—it was what they had come to believe was necessary. Some sins are like this. Our biggest challenge with such sins is figuring out how we were deluded into them in the first place. We need to know how we became vulnerable to being so mistaken so that we can avoid such vulnerabilities in the future. An example:

Diane is a beautiful woman inside and out, but her mother was cool and aloof with her all her life. When Diane found a young man whose mother adored her, she yielded to his sexual advances rather than risk losing him—and his mother. Diane berated herself for not saying no, but it was hard to resist feeling so loved. When she became pregnant and the young man and his mother both abandoned her, Diane was doubly devastated and sank into depression. When her father insisted that she have an abortion, Diane didn't resist.

It didn't take long for Diane to realize she had made terrible mistakes she would regret all her life and would never repeat, but it took years for her to sort out the hunger for love and the distorted thinking that had led her to give in to the unrighteous dominion of others. Her poor choices made it harder than ever for her to trust her own worth or basic goodness. But with the care and support of good bishops and good friends, Diane gradually learned to understand herself and her mother a little better, forgive her father and former boyfriend, and accept God's forgiveness. Complete self-forgiveness took time, but she continued to devote herself to service, radiating the goodness and beauty that were her truest identity.

People like Diane, once they have understood what made them vulnerable to sin, are not really tempted to repeat it. If anything, Diane's challenge was allowing herself to love and be loved and to freely participate as an equal partner in a lawful union. She is in the quadrant of Distrust, having changed her heart and behavior and now trying hard to trust that the forgiveness she has been offered by God and the Church is something she can also receive from others and herself.

While some serious sins are one-time events, other sins involve predispositions, habits, and addictions that are integrated into our bodies and minds. These require different kinds of change efforts. We can know our angry outbursts are wrong, but it may take time to retrain our reactions and learn new skills. While we may decry the damage our pornography addiction inflicts, rehabilitation is not just a matter of admitting fault. It takes honesty, consistent effort, doing

our homework, avoiding temptation, and getting help and support
to both humbly work on our weakness and fully repent for our sin.

Bruce sees the onset of his addiction as his first cigarette,
smoked at age nineteen. Within two years he had progressed
through alcohol, marijuana, and heroin, and then developed a serious addiction to crack cocaine. Only when he felt his life endangered
by a fellow drug dealer did he begin to realize the seriousness of
his situation. Because he had been raised in a good Latter-day Saint
home, the principles of the gospel were not foreign to him—just
very, very distant. Fleeing for his life, Bruce prayed for the first time
in months. He did not pray for his life to be spared. In fact, his life
was so out of control and his misery so acute that he didn't really
care if he died. He prayed only that God's will be done. As Bruce
turned his will over to God, an inexplicable peace filled his heart.
Bruce somehow knew he would live and that God wanted him back.

It took a year of struggle and ongoing effort before Bruce began
the period of lasting sobriety in which he now lives. During that year
Bruce took his parents and his bishop into his confidence, went
through periods of abstinence and relapse, got counseling and read
books, became active in the Church, and prayed continuously for
God's help. He learned about the Church's addiction-recovery program, began attending meetings, and found support from other
people with similar challenges. Even when he relapsed, he was able
to maintain hope because of constant reminders from others that
God loved and believed in him. He learned firsthand the power of
the Atonement and the efficacy of prayer, and these provided day-
by-day and sometimes minute-by-minute support.

A full change of behavior may take time, and we may continue
to falter. Seeing our relapses as opportunities for learning and
renewal instead of evidences of how hopeless we are helps us avoid
discouragement. But addictive habits and predispositions may

continue to tempt us even after a period of sobriety. This does not mean we have not fully repented or are too evil to change. Temptation is simply a fact of life. The key is learning to see temptation as a cue to calmly get support, exercise, get some sleep, seek out friends, go to work, sort the mail, walk the dog, nourish ourselves in the scriptures, do our home teaching, and pray for help—not as a cue to engage the high drama of struggle on our way to repeating our addiction.

The LDS Family Services' Addiction and Recovery Program has helped people with a wide variety of addictive behaviors. The Addiction Recovery Program guidebook was written with the support of Church leaders and mental health professionals by people who have suffered from addiction and who have recovered. Based on the twelve-step program of Alcoholics Anonymous, this interactive guidebook adds the vital dimension of the atonement of Jesus Christ and the principles of the gospel to help people make lasting change. Along with participation in Addiction Recovery groups, this book is a vital resource for putting the principles of repentance and the promise of the Atonement to work in our lives.

APOLOGIZE

It is appropriate that we feel awful when we recognize we've sinned. Telling others of our deep regret and asking forgiveness can help heal their wounds and ours. It is never too late, or too soon, to say we're sorry. Apologizing helps relieve the unfair burden we have placed on those who trusted us, making it easier for them to forgive us. Apologizing helps uphold the moral values we share, affirming to others that they can safely let us back in because we agree to the rules.

Insurance companies wanting to avoid lawsuits and payouts

used to insist that doctors not speak to the families of people who died or were injured after a medical error. They were afraid to admit to some wrongdoing the family would exploit for money. But studies have shown that families are less likely to sue, not more, when doctors sincerely apologize for errors. We all know doctors are human too, and we are more likely to forgive when they admit their fallibility, uphold our right to be upset, and share in our grief over what happened. Christ taught this principle when he encouraged us to "agree with thine adversary quickly, whiles thou art in the way with him; lest at any time the adversary deliver thee to the judge, and the judge deliver thee to the officer, and thou be cast into prison" (Matthew 5:25).

We should note that sometimes apologies are not welcomed by those from whom we seek forgiveness. When Robert overstepped a sexual boundary with his adult stepdaughter he felt terrible. He tried to apologize, but she was justifiably furious and unwilling to listen. He offered to pay for her therapy, agreed to therapy himself—anything to get back in her good graces. But she refused to attend family events, sent his letters back unopened, and gave him no opportunity to express his deep regret for his behavior. He felt desperate for her forgiveness.

Staying in the tension of being unforgiven is painful, but so is the tension of being betrayed by someone we trusted. Giving people time to be angry is part of paying the price for what we did instead of expecting them to let us off the hook when they are not yet convinced we can be trusted. When Robert respected his stepdaughter's need for time and distance and stopped pushing for reconciliation, she eventually started coming back to family events. As he remained courteous and conciliatory but respected her desire for distance, she gradually stopped fleeing whenever he walked into a room. Eventually Robert felt that her anger had subsided enough that he dared ask another family member to ask her if he could send her a brief letter, which she could open only when she felt ready. She agreed.

Robert composed a carefully worded apology fully acknowledging his inappropriate behavior, empathizing with her feelings of betrayal, affirming her right to be angry, offering to pay for any treatment she felt might help her heal, and expressing his hope that one day she would be able to forgive him. He made it clear that this should happen on her terms and as it felt comfortable to her.

Robert hoped his letter would restore the relationship, and he was very disappointed that his stepdaughter never responded to his letter, but he continued to be respectful of her need for distance and time. Many weeks later a photographer placed them together in a family group picture, and Robert was surprised when she was not only willing to stand next to him but also briefly smiled at him. He smiled back and then let her be. Over the next few months she began to interact with him briefly at family events, then started a few light conversations, then gradually allowed him back into her life. She never brought up the incident, so Robert respected that her need for control should take precedence over his desire for closure. Perhaps some day she will want to talk more directly about what happened, but not now.

In situations of serious sin, we may need to apologize more than once to make our sincerity felt and to cover all aspects of the harm we've caused. However, even when we have committed grave errors, we want to be careful not to swamp the other person with apologies that are more about our need than theirs. Overapologizing cheapens the act, making our apology more about gaining reassurance for ourselves than helping the one we hurt.

REBUILD TRUST

We should not expect others to trust us again when we cannot yet trust ourselves. Until we have demonstrated changed behavior over time, including when we are under stress, we should not expect trust from others. It is up to us to rebuild the trust and pick up the responsibility for vigilance. A recovering alcoholic who used to get furious when his wife tracked him down on his cell phone now volunteers his whereabouts and encourages her to call if she has any worry about where he is. He has gone from blaming her for her hypervigilance to being hypervigilant himself about helping her feel safe.

Nate, a young husband with same-sex attraction, found himself slipping into old preoccupations when stress mounted in his life. He admitted to his therapist that he was struggling, but he did not want his wife to worry and so told her that all was fine. She sensed that he was hiding something and had every reason to believe from his past behavior that what he was hiding was involvement with his old haunts.

Nate thought his wife would trust him only if he hid from her all reasons to be suspicious, but in fact she trusted him more when he admitted to her that he was tempted, asked for support, and discussed with her how to combat his temptations. Not all wives would respond this way, but Nate's wife needed to hear honest words about how he was handling temptation, not pretend words about having no temptations. Sure, Nate's wife would have loved to know that his same-sex attraction was a thing of the past, but they each knew better. She knew that hiding his real feelings and struggles just made him feel lonelier, which in turn made his attraction stronger. Only when she saw that Nate also distrusted hiding his feelings did she feel safe.

It took Nate a while to realize that he also hid from his wife because it gave him more room to slip. Increased honesty made him feel more constrained, less free to do what he wanted. But it also brought him and his wife closer, helping him find real satisfaction and intimacy in their relationship.

When we seek to rebuild trust, it can help to directly ask the person we offended what would help. What do they need from us to help them trust us more? While some people struggle to realize that there is simply nothing another human can do to make them feel as safe again, many will think of specific words they need to hear, acts they need to see, or emotions they need expressed to help restore trust. We should not submit to cruel or unusual punishment, but we should be willing to restrict our freedom or demonstrate contrition to help the person we hurt regain trust. We should also realize that rebuilding trust will take time.

ACCEPT FORGIVENESS

A brood mare sends a colt away from the safety of the fold when it misbehaves, but the mare always lets the colt know when it is free to come back. Even when God sends us away physically, He wants us back. He never loses His love and concern for us as His children. We came to earth to come to know God in ways we could not had we remained in a position of innocence about good and evil. Sin can alienate us from God so much that it is hard for us to imagine that He could still love us. We may wallow in the quadrant of Despair or Distrust, not thinking we are good enough to merit forgiveness. Instead, we need to move steadily toward the quadrant of Self-Forgiveness.

When Beth's eleven-year-old niece, Gina, stole a large sum of money from her purse, Beth confronted her calmly but firmly. Gina burst into tears and was almost inconsolable. In her young life, this was the most serious sin she could imagine. She was sure Beth would never trust her again and that she would never again be welcome in Beth's home. Beth calmly explained that she loved her very much and could see that Gina was sorry for what happened, but she wanted Gina to remember how bad she felt to help her not make this mistake again. Beth also told her that it would take some time for her to trust Gina again, that Gina would have to earn that trust, and that Beth would have to tell Gina's parents what had happened. Beth was not all that upset by this event, but she knew it was good that Gina was. It showed her that Gina's conscience was in place to help her in the future. Beth wanted to strengthen Gina's strong values while also strengthening Gina's image of herself as someone who lived up to those values.

Beth realized from this experience that perhaps God also was not as surprised by her own sins as she sometimes was, and that if she could still love Gina, God could certainly still love them both. Gina had never imagined that she could do something so bad, and she learned from this incident that she was fallible. But Gina had also never imagined that someone could still love her and want her around after she did something so bad, and she learned from this incident that her secure place in Beth's affections was big enough even to hold her mistakes.

Gina still has a choice to make. She can withdraw into shame and deny Beth's forgiveness, live down to her error, and refuse to ever feel trustworthy again. She can fight and rage to punish Beth for having the audacity to point out her theft and make her feel bad. She can refuse to come back to Beth's house because it is too humiliating to face her. Or she can tell Beth she is really sorry, accept that humility does not have to mean humiliation, and gently allow herself to forget what happened except when she needs it to remind herself of the value of honesty or the trustworthiness of Beth's love.

Paul wrote:

> Who shall separate us from the love of Christ? shall tribulation, or distress, or persecution, or famine, or nakedness, or peril, or sword? . . .
>
> Nay, in all these things we are more than conquerors through him that loved us.
>
> For I am persuaded, that neither death, nor life, nor angels, nor principalities, nor powers, nor things present, nor things to come,
>
> Nor height, nor depth, nor any other creature, shall be able to separate us from the love of God, which is in Christ Jesus our Lord (Romans 8:35, 37–39).

I could add: Neither sin, nor weakness, nor shame, nor anger, nor addiction, nor abuse, nor trauma, nor depression, nor selfishness, nor perfectionism, nor stealing money from our aunt's purse shall be able to separate us from the love of God, which is in Christ Jesus our Lord.

Elder Richard G. Scott of the Quorum of the Twelve Apostles said:

> Now if you are one who cannot forgive yourself for serious past transgressions—even when a judge in Israel has assured that you have properly repented—if you feel compelled to continually condemn yourself and suffer by frequently recalling the details of past errors, I plead with all of my soul that you ponder this statement of the Savior:
>
> "He who has repented of his sins, the same is forgiven, and I, the Lord, remember them no more.
>
> "By this ye may know if a man repenteth of his sins—

. . . he will confess them and forsake them." (D&C 58:42–43.)

To continue to suffer when there has been proper repentance is not prompted by the Savior but the master of deceit, whose goal is to bind and enslave you. Satan will press you to continue to relive the details of past mistakes, knowing that such thoughts make forgiveness seem unattainable. In this way Satan attempts to tie strings to the mind and body so that he can manipulate you like a puppet.

I testify that when a bishop or stake president has confirmed that your repentance is sufficient, know that your obedience has allowed the Atonement of Jesus Christ to satisfy the demands of justice for the laws you have broken. Therefore you are now free. Please believe it. To continually suffer the distressing effects of sin after adequate repentance, while not intended, is to deny the efficacy of the Savior's Atonement in your behalf.

When memory of prior mistakes encroached upon Ammon's mind, he turned his thoughts to Jesus Christ and the miracle of forgiveness. Then his suffering was replaced with joy, gratitude, and thanksgiving for the Savior's love and forgiveness (see Alma 26:17–20). Please, go and do likewise. Do it now so that you can enjoy peace of conscience and peace of mind with all their attendant blessings.[3]

12

FORGIVING OURSELVES
AS PARENTS

The Son of God hath atoned for original guilt,
wherein the sins of the parents cannot be answered
upon the heads of the children. . . .
And it is given unto them to know good from evil;
wherefore they are agents unto themselves. . . .
Wherefore teach it unto your children, that all
men, everywhere, must repent, or they can in
nowise inherit the kingdom of God. . . .
This is the plan of salvation unto all men,
through the blood of mine Only Begotten.

—MOSES 6:54, 56–57, 62

Parenting is one of those things that is so worth doing that it is worth doing imperfectly—which is how all parents do it. It is impossible to parent perfectly, yet there is no job we would rather do well. Those we love most suffer the most for our failures, and the consequences of our sins and weaknesses can spread throughout our children's lives and into future generations. Why would anyone sign up for such an undertaking! Indeed, we would be fools to do so were it not for the atonement of Jesus Christ.

No child has perfect parents; nor is that God's plan. Parental imperfections are part of the context of good and evil within which children exercise agency (Moses 6:55). Even our parental imperfections can help children learn, grow, develop compassion, and increase in faith. We try to trust this, but we may still wonder if our children would have been better off with someone else at the helm of their family ship. Parental guilt can be an especially heavy burden when children are mentally or physically ill, poor students, socially awkward, inactive in the Church, law breakers, suicidal, or when they have same-sex attractions, addictions, marital problems, or sexual struggles. Yet these situations touch almost every family.

The scriptures contain numerous stories of parents who ache for their children—Alma the Elder (Mosiah 27:14), Rebekah and Isaac (Genesis 26:34–35), David (2 Samuel 18:33), and others—but no stories in which parenting misdeeds are as dramatically forgiven as Alma the Younger's personal sins were. If we wait for a cleansing vision to relieve our parental guilt, we will probably be disappointed. But as we acknowledge our errors, change what we can, apologize sincerely and try to improve, we can make peace with our children and with our human limitations and weaknesses as parents. While we will always hurt to see our children struggle, we bless them as well as ourselves when we distinguish sins we have repented of from weaknesses we are humbly working on.

The gospel doesn't just give us a chance to be born again but to grow up again—to grow up in God. Joseph Smith prayed at the dedication of the Kirtland Temple that the Saints who worship there "may grow up in thee, and receive a fulness of the Holy Ghost, and be organized according to thy laws, and be prepared to obtain every needful thing" (D&C 109:15). I note with interest that the temple, which contains our most complex liturgy, is not focused on stories about the perfect life of Christ, but on the imperfect life of our first parents, and on how we too may repent and gain redemption even though we fall and sin. Christ is certainly represented in the temple—but as the Perfect One who instructs, atones, and saves, not as the Perfect One whose life we are expected to emulate in this life. Our endowment of power comes as we contemplate the gifts and opportunities that we can receive through both imperfect parents and a perfect Redeemer.

THE VALUE OF APOLOGIZING

This is all well and good, but I still feel awful when I see I'm not the patient, wise, invested, selfless parent I aspire to be. And that is when I imagine some white-clothed angel smiling beatifically and uttering the judicious and edifying words: Buck up!

I'm not sure where this expression comes from, but the gist of it seems to be to own up to our responsibility for something and not run away from it, to have the courage to face something hard—such as a human child. Those sweet babies look so innocent and helpless, but as they grow they can tax our every resource, spotlight our every flaw, and cause us to question everything we think we know about ourselves and life. We can wonder if we will ever feel like a competent adult at the end of our days or if we will spend life regretting our mistakes and stammering apologies. But competent adulthood is actually consistent with regret and apology, not antithetical to it. The most mature adults apologize freely, effectively, and sincerely. In fact, among the most important, healing, instructive, and loving things we can do as parents is to stammer apologies.

We can fall off either side of the horse when it comes to

apologizing to our children—the side of excessive, self-focused apologizing or inadequate, self-justifying apologizing. On the first side, excessive and self-focused apologizing, we are probably living in the quadrant of Distrust or Despair, not really believing in our own basic goodness or ability to qualify for forgiveness. We express so much shame or self-pity that our kids feel like bullies for ever bringing up a disagreement or hurt feeling. Excessive apology and self-blame for our parenting failures can send the message that mistakes (ours *or theirs*) are mortifying, catastrophic, and irreparable. We can inadvertently communicate that we think our kids turned out so poorly that we feel humiliated to the ground at what lousy parents we are. We can get them so worried about protecting us from feeling awful about our bad parenting that their own hurt feelings have to go underground. We can come across as martyrs who are too fragile to stand up to or too angelic to live up to. And we can be downright annoying.

When we make a mistake or do something hurtful as parents, our best course is to apologize sincerely and try to make it right. We should avoid going overboard with self-recrimination that leaves our children feeling like heels just for having feelings or that implies that perfection is our normal course of action except for a few rare and horrifying exceptions. Instead, we may simply need to *buck up*, accept that we are not above making mistakes, stop whining about how awful we are or how extenuating the circumstances, and focus attention instead on the feelings of the child we hurt.

The second side of the horse is to avoid apologizing because we don't like admitting our mistakes and want someone or something else to blame instead. We then are probably in the quadrant of Delusion, not wanting to look our mistakes square in the eye. We see apologizing as an admission of inferiority, not an acceptance of our inherent humanity and fallibility. We don't apologize because we don't want our children to think we don't know what we are doing (though we don't), that they don't have to listen to us (though they don't), or that we are not ideal parents (though we aren't). Admitting we are wrong can feel like giving our children a free pass to ignore us, blame us, or disrespect us. It isn't. Admitting we are wrong and sincerely apologizing is how we teach our children to also admit they are wrong and to sincerely apologize so they too may grow and learn.

Even if we humbly and sincerely apologize for either a weakness or a sin, there are many reasons our children may continue to blame us for our errors or their own. They may reject our apologies as too little too late ("I'm so sorry I missed your game again—I get so busy at work I just forget"). They may perceive apologies as veiled messages that we don't think they turned out very well and that *that* is what we are really sorry about ("I've made so many terrible mistakes as a parent—it's not your fault you're a terrible student"). They may simply need a little time to take in the implications of our apology and forgive.

Just because our children aren't ready to forgive us doesn't mean we have to keep beating our chests or give in to unreasonable demands. A child may not yet have the ego strength to accept an apology without milking it for all it's worth, but we can still remember that we are the grown-ups here. We can respond with humility, patience, and interest instead of requiring them to change before they are ready. Lecturing them—either about how wrong they are not to forgive us or about how worthless and pitiful we feel—is counterproductive.

I learned an invaluable lesson about the importance of apologizing with my son, who was about eight at the time. For several years he had had a bad habit of hitting when he got angry. We'd tried all the customary child-rearing techniques to get him to stop hitting but to no avail. In frustration I went to a colleague for advice, and he asked me where my son might have learned to hit when he was angry. I had no idea—we were certainly not a violent family. My colleague asked if I had spanked my son when he was younger. That stopped me cold. I had, and not always in that calm, collected manner that is supposedly appropriate (I'm no longer so sure how appropriate). My colleague pointed out that it sounded like my son had learned from me to hit when he was angry. This was not what I expected.

What was I to do? I had outgrown this poor parenting technique several years before, but apparently my son had not yet outgrown the bad lessons in anger management he had learned from me. My colleague made a simple suggestion: Apologize.

Apologize? I didn't want to apologize. It felt silly to apologize for something I hadn't done in years. Anyway, I was pretty sure my son would no longer even remember that I used to spank him, and I didn't really want to remind him. But as I began to think about the bad example I had set and the consequences it might be having, I began to see that even though I had changed my bad behavior, I still needed to complete the other steps of repentance. In fact, the more I thought about it the more I knew my colleague was right, and the worse I felt about hurting my son both in the past and probably in the present.

I had to prepare for my apology. I knew I needed to be humble and sincere (I was), and I also knew I needed to be prepared not to get defensive if he became angry or blaming. I also knew I did not want to get self-pitying or groveling about how awful I was in a way that would require him to worry about my feelings when I needed instead to be worried about his. I had to practice in my head for a couple of days, and I prayed for help to focus on his hurt and my bad behavior, not the other way around.

When I felt ready, I approached my son at bedtime and asked

if we could talk. I asked him if he remembered that sometimes I used to spank him when he was little. "Yes," he replied, looking suddenly quite resentful. Ouch. Wanting to know how he saw things, I asked him how often he remembered getting spanked. "Every day!" he pronounced. Ouch again. Apparently he had not forgotten after all. Not wanting to discount his feelings, I simply said (*very* meekly, I might add—as my goal was not to discount his feelings or defend what I had done), "I can sure imagine that it feels like you got spanked every day, but I promise it wasn't that often. But what I mostly want you to know is that I was wrong to spank you at all. I shouldn't have done that, and I'm really, really sorry. Spanking you was wrong. I should have known better, and I don't blame you for being mad at me. I hope you can forgive me." He didn't say a word but just sat there looking mad. I didn't know what else to say so I just repeated how sorry I was, said we could talk about this again if he wanted, and slunk out of his room.

And that was the end of my son's problem with hitting. I'm not kidding. No more hitting. Done. Finished. Over. And you'll notice I never even said a word about his behavior—only mine. I learned a powerful lesson about the importance of a sincere apology, even one given years later. Even when I think the other person is really the one with the problem that needs correcting, apologies for *our* wrong behavior are appropriate. Not all apologies will have this kind of impact, but effective and sincere apologies can make a difference for good.

What a blessing for all of us to live in a home where apologies are given and received! When we genuinely apologize, we not only merit our children's forgiveness but our own.

EFFECTIVE APOLOGIES

People who study apologies note that effective apologies have certain characteristics. While most of us are pretty good at spotting what is wrong with someone else's ineffective apology, many of us are not so good at apologizing in ways that promote mutual forgiveness, help us restore self-esteem after a failure, and help the other party let go. Psychiatrist Aaron Lazare has studied apologies extensively and notes that effective apologies correctly identify:

- ✦ to whom the apology is owed,
- ✦ the nature of the grievance from the other person's perspective,
- ✦ the impact on the offended party's feelings and well-being,
- ✦ the social or moral contract that was violated by the behavior.

In addition, the effective apologizer will usually express sincere remorse, make appropriate reparations, and give an honest explanation for the behavior.[1]

While not all of these steps have to happen every time, when our apology is not well received it probably misses on one or more of these factors. Chances are we are not conveying adequate humility, sincerity, empathy, remorse, or honesty. The good news is that we can try again. It is almost never too late to apologize, even to adult children, and effective apologies not only help the other person heal, but they also help us forgive ourselves.

Frank didn't feel very comfortable apologizing, but he could see that his teenage son, Josh, who never apologized to anyone, was getting on everyone's nerves. Frank concluded that perhaps Josh would benefit from a good example of apologizing, so Frank decided to give it a try. When Josh complained yet again that Frank was unfairly critical and demanding, Frank responded, "I'm sorry you find me so difficult. I guess you just have the bad luck of having a critical father who cares about you enough to try to help you improve. I apologize for ruining your life."

Josh was not very impressed with his father's apology and told him so, which left Frank convinced that Josh really was a miserable excuse for a kid if he could not even accept an apology. But after Frank cooled off he realized his apology was not really sincere, and he decided to try again. He thought through much more carefully what he wanted to say, waited for a quiet time, and asked Josh if they could talk. Then Frank said, "I've been giving a lot of thought to your complaint that I'm too critical, and I think you're right. Sometimes I want so much to help you do well that I don't give you a chance to figure things out before I jump in with suggestions. I can sure see why that wouldn't feel very good, and I don't blame you for being angry. I want to do better. I'm hoping you'll help me."

Josh was still angry, and he was unsure of his dad's sincerity. He replied with an unpleasant tone, "Oh, so now it's my job to help you be Mr. Nice Guy?"

Frank was determined to remain calm and friendly and said, "Josh, I know you're mad at me and I think I can understand why. I wouldn't expect you to forgive me all at once, but I hope you'll give me a chance to do better. I was wrong, and I'm so sorry. Dads are supposed to help their kids, and I've hurt you instead of helping you. I still want you to learn to do your best, but I need to find nicer ways to say it, and I need to give you a chance to figure things out without all my helpful suggestions. And I think I also need to let you know more how proud I am of you and how well you do a lot of things like pitching and history tests and helping your brother. Does that sound right?"

Softening a bit but still skeptical, Josh answered, "Yeah, that sounds right."

Frank said, "Okay, so at least we can agree on something! So how about we celebrate with some ice cream?"

Josh still held back. "I've got homework. I don't have time for ice cream."

Frank replied, "I can appreciate that. Maybe we can get ice cream another time. You're a great guy, Josh. I'm impressed that you are so conscientious about getting your homework done. And thanks for letting me talk. Okay if we talk more later?" Josh nodded ever so slightly, and then Frank left Josh to his suddenly very important homework.

It wasn't easy for Frank to stay calm when Josh was surly and unforgiving, but Frank worked hard to stay focused on his apology and not on Josh's response. He tried to remember that Josh's anger was a pretty good measure of how much he had been hurt—more than an indicator of what a rotten kid he was. Frank's second apology was more effective than the first one because he kept focused on his son's feelings and not his own. He described accurately how the situation might have felt to Josh, why it was wrong, and how he intended to change. He stayed calm, he realized that Josh was angry and didn't try to talk him out of it, and he gave Josh a chance to punish him a little for his bad behavior without criticizing him for it, demonstrating his sincere effort to be less critical. At first it felt a little humiliating to apologize because Frank wasn't totally sure he was even in the wrong, but he realized that if his own critical dad had apologized to him it would have really meant a lot to him. It felt good to begin to change an old and hurtful family pattern.

Lazare points out that an apology is not the end of the forgiveness process but the beginning of a negotiation between two parties with very different needs. People who have *been offended* need their feelings validated, their dignity restored, their sense of justice upheld, protection from further harm, assurance that the offending party upholds values both espouse, and evidence that the offender has suffered appropriately for the wrongdoing. In contrast, the person who has *given offense* needs relief from guilt or shame, restoration to society's good graces, the chance to learn from mistakes, reconciliation with important relationships, suspension of further punishment, and a renewal of self-esteem. When we fairly negotiate such a reconciliation, self-forgiveness follows more easily.

Frank's sincere apology was an opening bid for negotiating these competing needs. Josh may or may not be someone who will accept his dad's apology once he has time to let it sink in. If not, Frank can further this negotiation by remaining calm, curious, and conciliatory. He can ask Josh what he wants or needs in order for Frank to demonstrate sincerity and deserve forgiveness. Frank may not feel he can give Josh everything he wants, but if an apology fails to elicit forgiveness, then asking what the offended needs to make things right is at least a good next bid in the negotiation.

It isn't easy when we "lower" ourselves as parents, only to have our children keep us on the hook. Part of forgiving ourselves for being imperfect and human as parents is forgiving our children for being imperfect and human as children. We can't repent for our children; nor do they have to change for us to feel at peace with ourselves and God. But we can still repent, humble ourselves, apologize, and then pat ourselves on the back for developing such an important parenting skill.

BREAKING CYCLES OF INTERGENERATIONAL SIN AND WEAKNESS

As Frank thought about Josh's complaints, he realized that his own father's criticism had left him feeling insecure about his abilities and in turn nervous that his children would not measure up. This insecurity fueled his critical tendencies. Like many parents, Frank was doing what seemed normal and natural because it was what he saw and experienced at home, even though as a child he had felt its sting and known there had to be a better way. Each of us has the responsibility and opportunity as parents to improve on the weakness or sin of the past generation as we try our hand at the parenting wheel.

As we do so we can ask ourselves the simple question, "What did I need as a child that I didn't get?" Our answers might include such things as more honest explanations, more encouragement, less criticism, less expectation for perfection, more consistency, more help with homework, less involvement in parents' disputes, less hovering. As we try to answer this question we can try to figure out ways to give ourselves and our children more of those needed but missing emotional supplies while continuing the good in the legacy we received at home.

Often when we forgive ourselves for having been normal, ordinary children, rather than tirelessly trying to prove that our parents were wrong about our faults, we can also forgive our children for being normal, ordinary kids. There is something freeing about saying, "My dad was right! I was . . . (lazy, too sensitive, bad at math, slow, jealous of my sister, and so forth). And I still am! So what? This is not a capital offense that I must prove him wrong for believing. I can accept this about myself with a sense of humor and perspective."

Of course, sometimes parents *are* wrong about their children. Parents can think children are outrageous when they are just creative, lazy when they are just calm, or stupid when they simply have a learning disability. But often parents are right about children's characteristics—just wrong about their meaning. They see awkward stages and conclude a child is awkward as a permanent and perva-sive trait instead of realizing that all children (and adults!) are awk-ward sometimes and that this is not a cause for alarm or shame. They see laziness as a character flaw instead of as a reflection of healthy balance, normal immaturity, or a delightful capacity to enjoy the moment. They may feel threatened by ways their children are different from them (or like them!), seeing these characteristics as a reflection on their poor parenting and something they must point out and correct—when the child could really use a little more patience, acceptance, and enjoyment of who they are instead.

Our parents made these mistakes with us, sometimes wounding our self-image or failing to provide the help we needed. We do the same. There is no manual that makes it perfectly clear whether a child needs more correction or more acceptance, more tutoring or more medication, more hygiene reminders or more hugs. Our job is to try to learn from our parents' mistakes and our own and then go forward to listen a little more empathetically, help a little more patiently, try a little more consistently.

BUILDING ON STRENGTHS

We congratulate Frank for commenting positively on Josh's con-scientiousness about his homework (even if it reflected Josh's need to punish his dad rather than his real scholarly interests) and hope he will find more ways to affirm Josh's good choices, not just critique his mistakes. In a similar vein, we hope Frank will congratulate him-self for trying again to apologize and for taking this task so seriously. Frank is more than a "critical parent"; he also learns from his mis-takes, puts his son's feelings above his own comfort, and keeps his cool when his son is angry. Frank has a lot of parenting strengths.

While all parents have weaknesses that affect their children, few parents *only* mess up their children. We also listen to them, teach them, try to help them, support them, provide for them, and protect them—at least some of the time. As important as it is to work on correcting our parenting mistakes, we also need to remember and focus on our parenting strengths. Unless we are involved with serious parenting sins like physical, emotional, or sexual abuse or severe neglect, building on our strengths as parents is probably much more important than eliminating every weakness. Likewise, helping our children to build on their strengths is probably more important than correcting every flaw.

What are your strengths as a parent? Note that you do not have to be actively engaged in producing art all the time to consider yourself artistic, nor do you have to be thoughtful or cheerful all the time to claim these as strengths. Circle two or three strengths you *generally* have as a parent. Check two or three strengths your parents had. Think of someone you consider a good parent and put that parent's initials by the traits you think make them good parents. Add other traits or skills not listed here.

I notice that people I think of as being excellent parents do not possess every strength on this list, nor do they all have the same strengths. They generally do a few things well, show a sincere interest in their children, and work to neutralize their more glaring weaknesses. We move toward the quadrant of Self-acceptance as we humbly develop our strengths and work patiently on our weaknesses, praying for God's grace to help us.

Patient	Thoughtful
Friendly	Independent
Affectionate	Consistent
Curious	Invested in family
Interested in others	High-achieving
Sense of humor	Helpful
Forgiving	Health-conscious
Orderly	Prayerful
Hard-working	Fun-loving
Cheerful	Protective
Humble	Artistic
Fair	Musical
Compassionate	Creative
Affirming	Athletic
Flexible	Good provider
Self-sacrificing	Appreciative
Service-oriented	Honest
Happy	Good listener
Sincere	Wise
Spiritually oriented	Balanced
Love learning	Supportive
Persistent	Disciplined
Easygoing	_____
Encouraging	_____

AGENTS UNTO THEMSELVES

I also note that some people I consider excellent parents have children who struggle, and some people I consider mediocre parents have children who are exceptional. Children are not just reflections of their parents' virtues and vices; they are agents unto themselves, acting and not just being acted upon. There is a time for soul-searching when our children make choices we disagree with and a time to accept that the plan of salvation is a plan of agency.

When Felicity's son stopped going to church, Felicity was devastated. She had made great sacrifices for her faith, and her son's choices rocked her world. She fasted weekly for many months, prayed with desperation and tears for God to help her child, and did a lot of soul-searching for her parenting mistakes. Then, at the beginning of a new year, she sat down to record her goals and plans for the future. She began to automatically write down "fast every Sunday," when the spiritual impression came, unbidden: "The time for fasting and grief is over now. It is time to stop grieving for the son you lost and time to start rejoicing in the son you have." She did not feel any rebuke in this notion—rather a validation that while our prayers of desperation and fear are heard by God, there is a time to replace them with prayers of gratitude and trust. There is a time to stop grieving for what is wrong and start rejoicing in what is yet right and strong and good in our children, in us, and—even when all else fails—in God's great plan of salvation and happiness. The Lord knows and loves our children far better than we, and we can afford to put both their lives and ours in His able hands.

NOT HOLDING BACK

Recently I found myself in a familiar place of helplessness and angst over difficult decisions and projects my adult children faced. I was also worrying about my parents, who need more care than they are comfortable accepting. In addition, some important personal matters affecting my future loomed beyond my control. As I prayed for the thousandth time for help with these situations, I found myself reflecting on the story of Ananias and Sapphira in

Acts 5—a story I've never been comfortable with but that I was sup-posed to teach in Sunday School that week. This is the story of two members in the early Church who sold a piece of property and brought their earnings to the apostles as an act of consecration, but they secretly kept back part of the price. When Peter discerned their deception and called them on it, each of them fell over dead in shock. Needless to say, everyone who witnessed this was terrified at what they observed.

This story suggests impressive discernment on the part of the chief apostle and demonstrates the importance of honesty with God, both of which I appreciate. Still, this story has always scared and bothered me. Is this how God is—waiting to catch me in a moment of weakness if I don't do everything perfectly? What happened to the God of love and forgiveness and mercy? If this is what it takes to be a disciple of Christ, I'm in real trouble.

As my worries intersected with my Sunday School lesson, I felt something very different in this story, however. Instead of a never-satisfied God shaking His finger at my selfishness, I felt God reaching out His hand to me, asking me to give Him everything—my children, my parents, my worries—and to trust that He would both give me back the portion that would be for my blessing and tenderly care for the rest. I realized that when we hold back from God, something in us will start to die. We do not just struggle to give Him our assets; we also struggle to give Him our deficits. His request that we give Him everything—holding nothing back—can be a great blessing.

Our children are among the precious blessings we are to con-secrate to God, and the more difficult they are or the more out of our control, the more that consecration is necessary to both them and us. Of course this doesn't mean that we wash our hands of our offspring and walk away. It is tricky to both invest deeply in our children and stop investing our self-esteem and sense of well-being in their decisions. But I think there is a lesson for me in the story of Ananias and Sapphira: when I claim that everything I have is God's but I hold back a part to worry about and turn into a statement about me instead, then I am the one who pays for my self-deception. A child is a stewardship whose needs we are accountable to help meet, not a possession we use to meet *our* needs for security or worth.

NEVER GIVE UP

We've probably all heard the counsel to never give up on a child. It can be even harder not to give up on ourselves. But when we give up on ourselves as parents, we communicate to our children that their failures are too much for us to handle, too devastating for us to accommodate—which is not too different from saying that they have failed too much to be forgiven. Not only is this not helpful, but it is also not true—neither about them nor about us.

When I am tempted to believe that my mistakes as a parent are too much to accept, I remember a story I read decades ago that has stuck in my mind ever since, even though I had long since forgotten where or when I read it until I went to some lengths to locate it a few years ago. It is a story of Dr. Russell M. Nelson, who was a pioneer in open-heart surgery. It provides a vivid example of a crucial point all parents need to grasp. I invite you to read it carefully, taking in all the details, pausing to imagine the feelings of all the parties involved.

In 1957, Brother and Sister H. brought their third child to me for repair of congenital heart disease. Their first child had died from congenital heart disease before the advent of cardiac surgery, and their second also died after an unsuccessful open-heart operation that I performed. I operated on the third child, but she died later that night.

My grief was beyond expression. When I went home, I told the story to Dantzel [my wife] and said, "I'm through. I'll never do another heart operation as long as I live!" I wept most of the night. All I could think of were the faces of those two parents, and I could still see those pathetic children in my mind, blue-lipped and with clubbed fingers, yet with smiles of confidence and hope. I determined that my inadequacies would never be inflicted on another human family.

When morning came, Dantzel finally said, "Isn't it better to keep trying than to quit now and require others to go through the same grief of learning what you already know?"

I listened to her counsel. I returned to the laboratory to work a little harder, learn a little more, and strive further.[2]

This story speaks of the pain of a surgeon who could not save a life but who had learned too much about his craft the hard way to give up just because it was devastating to face how much he still did not know. But to me this is also the story of what it means to be a parent, especially a parent who is trying to be a good parent, as we attempt to navigate the uncharted seas of our children's hearts. We have little training for this job. The risks are many, the price of failure high, and despite our best intentions we simply cannot know enough to always perform our delicate tasks correctly. Yes, we will often fail. Yes, we may wish we could quit so as to not face the indignity and grief of failing at something that counts so much, that matters so deeply. But implicit in this story is another story—the story of the saving power of Christ to both resurrect the dead and redeem the living—a power that means we can afford to keep trying even if we will often fail because He will eventually triumph, and our failures can be redeemed by His victory.

We cannot afford to give up on ourselves as parents. The people we can help save if we learn from our errors and try to improve are too important to give up on. Some of our children may not be reachable in this life. Some will slip through our fingers despite our best efforts. Some will respond only to unproven techniques we must innovate, improve, and test as we go, techniques we may not discover in time to help them. But even our Father trusts fully in the atonement of His Son, the pivotal act on which His great plan of happiness turns. So can we.

The surgeon's story is all the more powerful to me because it is from the life of Elder Russell M. Nelson, who became an apostle of the Lord. No one is exempt from the pain of failing at something of life-and-death import except those who leave the most important tasks of mortality to others out of fear of failure. God does not reject us for failing. But He does ask us to buck up to the task of learning from our failures, mourning our losses, apologizing for our mistakes, getting help with our setbacks, and thoughtfully, prayerfully, trying again.

We can afford the risks of mortality, including the risk of failing as a parent, precisely because Christ atoned for our sins and for the sins of our children. We qualify for that gift as we grow up enough to face our failures, go back to the laboratory of the family and try again, and never give up on ourselves or those in our stewardship. Forgiving our children for being less than perfect, forgiving ourselves for having been less than perfect children, forgiving our parents, and forgiving our parenting failures—all of these go hand in hand as we strive to give our hearts to Christ, our eyes full of trust and hope.

13

BELIEVING GOD

But if the wicked will turn from all his sins that he hath
committed, and keep all my statutes, and do that which is
lawful and right, he shall surely live, he shall not die.
All his transgressions that he hath committed, they shall
not be mentioned unto him: in his righteousness that he
hath done he shall live.

—EZEKIEL 18:21–22

As part of the temple recommend interview, Church members are asked, "Do you have a testimony of the atonement of Jesus Christ and of His role as Savior and Redeemer?" Gaining and trusting such a testimony is at the heart of Christian discipleship. The meaning and purpose of life hinges on this central doctrine.

As we seek to claim the grace made possible through Christ's atonement, we are awed by the goodness of God's plan, the reach of His love. We become more humble, compassionate, and motivated by righteous desires. We pray to know that we have been forgiven, our sins remitted. Answers to such prayers will not generally come in dramatic ways but by quiet assurances and gentle reminders of God's love and confidence in us. Sometimes we will receive impressions of more we need to change, additional apologies to make, or other lessons to acquire before forgiveness is granted. We can continue to ask, "Please help me to see my sins so I can repent." Or "Please help me know which of my weaknesses to tackle next and how to better serve from my strengths." Or "Please help me know and feel that my repentance is accepted and that I can now move on."

This book has suggested steps in a process that can lead to such self-forgiveness and self-acceptance. They include clarifying our doctrinal understanding and personal philosophy about the purpose of life and the difference between sin and weakness, taking the necessary steps of repentance, beginning to address the personality styles that complicate self-forgiveness, and tackling big-ticket sins and parenting flaws. However, even after we have worked through these steps, self-forgiveness does not automatically follow. When we still chafe at our own misdeeds, some of us will wonder if the chafing itself signifies that we are simply lesser souls. Some of us may wonder if the promise of forgiveness really applies to us or if, despite our repentance, our failures and weaknesses will yet catch up with us on Judgment Day. We may assume that others do not struggle as we do because they are simply better people. We may see new bouts of guilt and shame as evidence that we can never get beyond the reach of our past. We may stay stuck in Distrust or Despair.

There is yet another challenge that faces us as we wrestle with self-forgiveness or self-acceptance, and that is how to manage recurring reminders of our sins or weaknesses and the shame, guilt, anxiety, and hopelessness they may prompt. As we seek to replace self-talk focused on our failings and faults with self-talk focused on the Lord's forgiveness and mercy, we come to accept that the peace God offers may not be continuous (constant, unbroken, and uninterrupted), but it *is* continual (recurrent, repeated, and persistent).

So what do we do when moments of self-doubt or self-blame plague us? We make a decision—a decision to believe God even in the midst of self-doubt, a decision to distract ourselves from self-talk that tears us down and choose instead to trust in God's mercy and kindness and love. This is not a risk-free decision for the natural man. What if we have not yet done enough to make up for our bad attitude, our begrudging service? What if forgiveness is really the booby prize, and perfection, or at least something much closer to it, is really the goal? What if we are kidding ourselves about the severity of our sin? What if the weaknesses we have yet to overcome really do matter far more than whatever good we have tried to offer? What if we are wrong about God's grace being sufficient? What if we really cannot trust that there is goodness at the deepest core of who we are?

Harry Potter, the boy wizard of recent literary fame, faces such a question. He realizes in a moment of near-defeat that his anger, desires for power, and capacity to hurt others are not unlike the traits of the evil adversary he has tried to expose. His enemy, He-Who-Must-Not-Be-Named, taunts Harry with Harry's capacity for evil, encouraging him to accept the inevitability of giving in to this dark side. But Harry's wise and powerful mentor reminds him that it is not the ways Harry is like his enemy that are important because we all have the capacity for evil. What matters is how Harry is different. Harry also has the demonstrated capacity for love, loyalty, compassion, empathy, kindness, and the righteous use of power. Harry resists evil and desires good, unlike He-Who-Must-Not-Be-Named. This is what defines him, setting him apart from the evil one.

This is what "sets us apart" as well, in every sense of these words.

To be sure, we too have dark capacities that we fear to name or acknowledge. We hope others will never see this dreaded self; in fact, we hope it does not really exist. Seeing our sins or weaknesses can threaten our ideal self-image, causing us to wonder if the dark self we fear is really who we most deeply are. In our moments of greatest self-doubt, we too need the wisest part of us to remember how we are more than our "self-as-feared."[1] We too have demonstrated capacities for love, service, self-discipline, and goodness. Our capacity for evil does not define us; our choices, intentions, and actions are the best measure of our truest self. This essential truth is hard to hold when Satan pulls out every stop to wring hope out of us.

The specter of the self-as-feared can spook us into thinking we must be truly evil if old sins still tempt us or old regrets still haunt us. Consider: Just because we have a sweet spiritual witness of the Church's truthfulness does not mean we will never doubt or dislike anything about the Church again; likewise, just because we have a sweet witness of God's forgiveness does not mean we will never again dislike that we have sinned. Just because we love a spouse or child or friend does not mean we will never disapprove of them; just because we forgive ourselves does not mean we will never again feel bad for past failures or sad for those we've hurt. With a testimony, we make the choice to hold on to a spiritual witness even when the spiritual intensity of the moment passes. With a committed relationship, we make the choice to hold on to our partner or child or friend even when our loving feelings wax and wane. And with forgiveness, we make the choice to believe God's forgiveness even when old self-doubts or feelings of shame are triggered by new events or old memories. Self-forgiveness is not a constant state but a choice and exercise of our agency to believe God even when the witness of the Spirit is contradicted by the feelings of the moment.

Scriptural examples such as Alma or Nephi demonstrate that even great prophets can later doubt their goodness, regret sins for which they have been forgiven, and feel pain over repented-of failures. They have still been forgiven. Sadness over past mistakes is part of the price we pay to grow, change, and learn good from evil. We can accept such sadness and then gently turn back to what we felt from the Spirit to be true when we were closest to it. We can choose as an act of will to trust in God's power to redeem our misused agency (His plan) and ignore Satan's insistence that only perfection will do (his plan). We are not meant to live with consistent certainty in this life but by faith in our Father's love, wisdom, goodness, and promises.

The process of self-forgiveness is just that: a process. It is a way of traveling more than a place we arrive at. That we need to revisit steps in this process is not a sign that we or the process have failed but that we have more to learn from the experiences of mortality and the tutoring of the Spirit. Forgiving ourselves is a choice, an art, an act of trust in one of God's greatest promises: to bring us home.

The courage necessary to enact such a choice is illustrated by Christian writer Linda Dillow. She asks us to imagine ourselves among a group of spectators watching a man push a large St. Bernard dog in a wheelbarrow across a tightrope over Niagara Falls. The man balances skillfully, moving back and forth across the falls more than once with the dog. The crowd is impressed. He asks the spectators, "So do you think I could push a person across the falls in this wheelbarrow?" You and the rest of the crowd nod affirmatively— after all, a person weighs less and would be even more likely to hold still and cooperate with this process than the dog. Then the man turns, looks you in the eyes, and says, "Get in."[2]

This story illustrates well the challenge of the disciple of Christ.

It is one thing to believe that Christ can save and forgive the world but quite another to trust Him to save and forgive us. It feels like so much is at stake. What if we bet our lives on God's mercy and we are wrong? What if we have not yet done enough to merit His grace and we end up tumbling over the falls? This is a central task of mortality—to *practice trust* in God's goodness, power, and desire to save us.

I love the story of the brother of Jared in the Book of Mormon. The brother of Jared sees the finger of the premortal Christ touch some small stones to make them shine—a spectacular vision in answer to the brother of Jared's prayer for light for the long journey ahead. The brother of Jared falls down in fear at this unprecedented sight but then asks Christ to reveal Himself in full. Then Christ asks the brother of Jared a most unexpected question: Will you believe the words that I shall speak? (Ether 3:11). *Of course!* we all think. Who would doubt God's words under such circumstances? We assume that belief would be a given at this point in the story, following automatically from the events just witnessed. But this question reminds us that even for those who have seen spectacular visions, belief is a choice. The brother of Jared replies that he will believe because he knows that Jesus Christ is a God of truth and cannot lie. Christ in turn replies that because of this knowledge the brother of Jared is "redeemed from the fall" and therefore brought back into His presence; therefore Jesus shows Himself to him (v. 13). The choice to believe Christ is redemptive. It brings us close to God. It allows us to see who He really is and know Him as the God of love and truth. And it is always a choice.

In the council in heaven, we affirmed our support of the Father's plan of agency—agency we as well as others will inevitably misuse. Self-forgiveness requires us to sustain this plan again—here— both by taking the risks to use our agency and by trusting the provisions God has made for our redemption. Ultimately we choose to believe in God's grace out of desire and faith, not convincing arguments. We choose to believe despite our doubts, not by eliminating them. We choose to get in the wheelbarrow because there is simply no other way to get across the Fall, and God lives on the other side.

In the Garden of Eden the tree of life was always available—the tree representing God's absolute love, the tree whose fruit gave life. Once Adam and Eve transgressed God's law, God blocked the path to the tree of life lest they try to turn back the clock on their sudden mortality, defying death before repentance and faith in Christ could save them from their sins. For us too, the path to God does not permit return to the innocent state we were in before we knew we could sin. The way is forward.

We mourn our own demise. We may long to turn back the clock and un-know our dark side. Astoundingly, the Book of Mormon affirms in Lehi's dream that the tree of life we seek is not in the garden of innocence but in the midst of the dreary world, beyond the mists of darkness, past the river of filthy water, under the gaze and mocking fingers of the pride of the world (1 Nephi 8). This is where God's love for His children shines most brightly, beckoning us to partake in full trust and without shame.

In visions of the last days, Ezekiel (Ezekiel 47:1–12) and John the Revelator (Revelation 22:1–6) each saw a mighty river flow from the temple of God to heal the Dead Sea. This great river of living water nourished wondrous trees on both sides of its banks—trees whose leaves were for the healing of the nations and which gave fruit in every season to nourish the world. I believe there is a powerful message for us in these visions and that they do not refer only to the millennial day. I believe God not only wants us to partake of the tree of life but also to become trees of life, full of healing and nourishment for others and nurtured by the Living Water that is Jesus Christ. Today, now, life and healing flow from temple altars where we covenant to be God's people and He covenants to be our God. That Living Water, if we partake of it, heals our dead, desert places and lets us live, flourish, and feed others.

Living Water has a specific meaning in Judaism. It is water with both a source and an outlet. Our own dead seas are dead in part because we block and restrict them by our unwillingness to let go of our sins and resolve our regrets. A huge dead sea in which nothing can live is formed when we will not stop weeping salty tears for our abandoned sins. New life flows into us from the Savior as we partake of His healing power, plant the seed of faith in His atonement and love, and nourish that seed with the Living Water of His grace. Everlasting life, eternal life, can be ours even now as we, with the brother of Jared, choose to trust that He is a God of truth who cannot lie.

> For the mountains shall depart and the hills be removed, but my kindness shall not depart from thee, neither shall the covenant of my peace be removed, saith the Lord that hath mercy on thee (3 Nephi 22:10).

> For I am able to make you holy, and your sins are forgiven you (D&C 60:7).

ACKNOWLEDGMENTS

Now that you've read this book, let me tell you who to blame if you feel like you wasted your money: me. And let me tell you who to thank if you've found it helpful.

First, thank Dave Ulrich, Allen Bergin, and Christine Packard for reading, commenting on, and improving the entire manuscript. Dave's organizational capability, Allen's internationally renowned expertise in all things psychological, and Chris's editorial instinct and therapeutic sensitivity all contributed enormously to the readability and usability of this material.

Next, thank Christine Packard and Carrie Kelley, my colleagues and cofounders of Sixteen Stones Center for Growth, for being wise and compassionate counselors and therapists from whom I learn so much. Also thank the Association of Mormon Counselors and Psychotherapists for providing the primary forum in which I have developed my professional ideas over many years.

Then thank my parents, Les and Barbara Woolsey, for teaching me about apologies, forgiveness, and the inestimable value of good but imperfect parents in raising good but imperfect children. And while you are at it, thank my children, Carrie, Monika, and Michael, for patiently receiving me, tutoring me in both gospel and secular truths, making me laugh, and giving me something to practice on.

Thank Kathleen Flake and Karen Blake for walking the road with me, each in her own way. What would we do without true friends who love us anyway?

Of course thank Cory Maxwell at Deseret Book for taking a chance on an unknown author with an undeveloped idea. And thank Jay Parry, my conscientious editor, and the design and technical staff at Deseret Book for their creativity and expertise throughout the process of writing, rewriting, and bringing this book to fruition.

Be sure to thank my many clients (who can't be named but whose faces are dear to me and whose lives have inspired and instructed me), colleagues (especially David Klimek, Scott Gordon, Scott Richards, and Richard Ferre), missionaries (especially from the Canada Montreal Mission), friends (especially, but in no particular order, Moni, Linda, Paula, Ann, Mija, Susan, Nancy, Wayne, Helen, Harvey, Thom, Bonnie, John, Marci, Ginger, Kathie, Lynn, Rand, Matt, and Lucille), family members (especially Carla, Eric, Richard, Karin, Belinda, Melanie, David, and Kapka), and fellow Saints (especially Byron, Diane, Mark, Judy, Sondra, Polly, Linda, Betsy, Kris, and Sylvia) who have shared their stories with me and helped me create my own.

And finally come around again to thank Dave Ulrich, my husband, best friend, and—next to God—my most bountiful forgiver.

NOTES

Introduction: The Challenge

1. Gordon B. Hinckley, *Faith: The Essence of True Religion* (Salt Lake City: Deseret Book, 1989), 35.

Chapter 1: The Spiritual Basis for Self-Forgiveness

1. LDS Bible Dictionary, s.v. "Fear," 672.

2. Ibid., s.v. "Repentance," 760.

3. Julia Cameron, *The Artist's Way: A Spiritual Path to Higher Creativity* (New York: Putnam, 1992), 121.

4. James E. Faulconer, *Scripture Study: Tools and Suggestions* (Provo, Utah: FARMS, 1999), 148–49.

Chapter 2: Defining Self-Forgiveness

1. Boyd K. Packer, "The Brilliant Morning of Forgiveness," *Ensign*, November 1995, 19–20.

2. LDS Bible Dictionary, s.v. "Grace," 697.

3. Ibid.

4. Dallin H. Oaks, "Sins and Mistakes," *Ensign*, October 1996, 67.

CHAPTER 3: RECEIVING THE GIFT

1. *Webster's New World Compact School and Office Dictionary,* Victoria Neufeldt, ed. (New York: Simon and Schuster, 1995), 236.

2. This list is adapted in part from Beverly Flanigan, *Forgiving Yourself: A Step-by-Step Guide to Making Peace with Your Mistakes and Getting On with Your Life* (New York: Macmillan, 1996), 57–58.

CHAPTER 4: WHO DONE IT?

1. Desmond Tutu, *No Future Without Forgiveness* (New York: Doubleday, 1999), 270–71; Desmond Tutu, "Without Forgiveness There Is No Future," in Robert D. Enright and Joanna North, eds., *Exploring Forgiveness* (Madison: University of Wisconsin Press, 1998), xiii.

2. Other exercises on determining responsibility and self-forgiveness are found in Beverly Flanigan's *Forgiving Yourself* (New York: Macmillan, 1996), and Flanigan's *Forgiving the Unforgivable: Overcoming the Bitter Legacy of Intimate Wounds* (New York: Collier Books, 1992), from which some of the exercises in this chapter are adapted.

CHAPTER 5: REPENTANCE

1. LDS Bible Dictionary, s.v. "Repentance," 760.

2. When reasonable people find it unreasonably difficult to change despite desire, faith, scripture study, priesthood blessings, and concerted effort, they may benefit from some of the secular research on what leads to successful change. Such information can supplement the essential and primary spiritual guidance of the gospel and Church leaders. Good counselors, therapists, and medical doctors can help us apply this research to our situation.

3. The path of repentance and change, complete with both chutes and ladders, includes predictable steps that other books elaborate. See, for example, James O. Prochaska, John C. Norcross, and Carlo C. DiClemente, *Changing for Good: A Revolutionary Six-Stage Program for Overcoming Bad Habits and Moving Your Life Positively Forward* (New

York: Avon, 1994); LDS Family Services, *Addiction Recovery Program: A Guide to Addiction Recovery and Healing* (Salt Lake City: The Church of Jesus Christ of Latter-day Saints, 2005); Dennis Greenberger and Christine A. Padesky, *Mind over Mood: Change How You Feel by Changing the Way You Think* (New York: Guilford Press, 1995).

4. Prochaska, Norcross, and DiClemente, *Changing for Good*, 48.

5. Ibid., 113–15.

6. Ibid., 145–49.

7. See Malcolm Gladwell, *The Tipping Point: How Little Things Can Make a Big Difference* (Boston: Little, Brown and Co., 2000).

8. Deliberate murder is a special case not dealt with here.

9. Carrie L. Kelley, "Understanding the Experiences of LDS Women with Same-sex Attraction," (doctoral dissertation, California School of Professional Psychology, 2002), 97.

10. Gary Chapman and Jennifer Thomas, *The Five Languages of Apology: How to Experience Healing in All Your Relationships* (Chicago: Northfield Publishing, 2006), table of contents.

11. Neal A. Maxwell, "Repentance," *Ensign*, November 1991, 31.

12. See Beverly Flanigan, *Forgiving the Unforgivable: Overcoming the Bitter Legacy of Intimate Wounds* (New York: Collier Books, 1992); and Janis Abrahms Spring, *How Can I Forgive You? The Courage to Forgive, the Freedom Not To* (New York: Harper Collins, 2004).

13. Quoted in Julia Cameron, with Mark Bryan, *The Artist's Way* (New York: G.P. Putnam's Sons, 1992), 28.

14. LDS Bible Dictionary, s.v. "Fear," 672.

CHAPTER 6: SHAME AND PRIDE

1. Frederick Turner, "Shame, Beauty, and the Tragic View of History," *American Behavioral Scientist* 38 (August 1995): 1073.

CHAPTER 7: DEPRESSION

1. Anne Morrow Lindbergh, *Gift from the Sea* (New York: Pantheon, 1997), 124.

2. See David D. Burns, *Feeling Good: The New Mood Therapy* (New York: Collins, 1999); Dennis Greenberger and Christine Padesky, *Mind over Mood: Change How You Feel by Changing the Way You Think* (New York: Guilford Press, 1995).

3. Clinical depression is also generally treatable. Both medication and psychotherapy provide relief for many with clinical depression.

4. See Wendy Ulrich, "Identification and Referral of Depressed Secondary School Students," (doctoral dissertation, University of Michigan, 1989).

5. Mark Twain, *The Adventures of Huckleberry Finn* (New York: Bantam Books, 1981), 205.

6. Mihaly Csikszentmihalyi, *Flow: The Psychology of Optimal Experience* (New York: Harper & Row, 1990), 6.

7. Marion D. Hanks, "He Means Me," *Ensign*, May 1979, 74, 76.

8. Lindbergh, *Gift from the Sea*, 124.

CHAPTER 8: ANXIOUS PERFECTIONISM

1. Allan E. Mallinger and Jeannette De Wyze, *Too Perfect: When Being in Control Gets Out of Control* (New York: Random House, 1992), 14–15, 38.

2. Julia Cameron, *The Artist's Way: A Spiritual Path to Higher Creativity* (New York: Putnam, 1992), 120.

3. Bruce C. Hafen, *The Broken Heart: Applying the Atonement to Life's Experiences* (Salt Lake City: Deseret Book, 1989), 113–14.

CHAPTER 9: SELF-DESTRUCTIVE UNSELFISHNESS

1. Harriet Goldhor Lerner, *The Dance of Anger* (New York: Harper & Row, 1997), 17–18.

CHAPTER 10: TRAUMA AND ABUSE

1. See Lenore Terr, *Too Scared to Cry: Psychic Trauma in Childhood* (New York: Harper & Row, 1990).

CHAPTER 11: THOUGH YOUR SINS BE AS SCARLET

1. Bruce C. Hafen, "Beauty for Ashes: The Atonement of Jesus Christ," *Ensign*, April 1990, 7.

2. James A. Cullimore, "Confession and Forsaking: Elements of Genuine Repentance," *Ensign*, December 1971, 87.

3. Richard G. Scott, "Peace of Conscience and Peace of Mind," *Ensign*, November 2004, 17–18.

CHAPTER 12: FORGIVING OURSELVES AS PARENTS

1. Aaron Lazare, *On Apology* (New York: Oxford University Press, 2004), 75, 107.

2. Lane Johnson, "Russell M. Nelson: A Study in Obedience," *Ensign*, August 1982, 21.

CHAPTER 13: BELIEVING GOD

1. Beverly Flanigan, *Forgiving Yourself: A Step-by-Step Guide to Making Peace with Your Mistakes and Getting On with Your Life* (New York: Macmillan, 1996), 47.

2. Linda Dillow, *Calm My Anxious Heart* (Colorado Springs, Colo.: NavPress, 1998), 135–36.

INDEX